The Authentic Doctrine of the Eucharist

Teresa Whalen

Sheed & Ward

Sheed & Ward™ is a service of The National Catholic Reporter Publishing Company.

Library of Congress Cataloguing-in-Publication Data

Whalen, Teresa, 1963-
    The authentic doctrine of the Eucharist / by Teresa Whalen
       p.   cm.
    Includes bibliographical references and index.
    ISBN 1-55612-558-5 (acid-free)
    1. Lord's Supper--Catholic Church. 2. Catholic Church--Doctrines.
I. Title.
IN PROCESS
234'.163--dc20   92-21577
                                                CIP

Published by: Sheed & Ward
                 115 E. Armour Blvd.
                 P.O. Box 419492
                 Kansas City, MO 64141-6492

To order, call: (800) 333-7373

Contents

Introduction

THE EUCHARIST IS, AND ALWAYS HAS BEEN, THE CENTRAL act of worship for Roman Catholics.[1] As a result, the desire to reach a proper understanding of the meaning of the eucharist has dominated much of Roman Catholic sacramental theology throughout the centuries. In order to be able to authentically celebrate that sacrament which Christ instituted at the Last Supper, Catholics need to have a full understanding of the meaning behind it. From the very beginnings of the early Church right up until the present day, this quest for meaning has been manifest in the controversies that have raged and are raging over the correct understanding of the sacrament. While the point of the disputes has often varied, one thing has remained the same: all were without doubt concerned with the proper meaning and authentic celebration of the eucharist.

In the earliest Christian times, the eucharist was celebrated simply and informally as part of an ordinary meal. Even at this early time, however, there is evidence of this concern for a meaningful celebration of the eucharist. To the Corinthians, St. Paul writes:

> When you meet together, it is not the Lord's Supper
> that you eat. For in eating, each one goes ahead with
> his own meal, and one is hungry and another drunk . . .
> For anyone who eats and drinks without discerning the
> body eats and drinks judgement upon himself . . . (RSV
> I Corinthians 11: 20-21, 29)

According to the Pauline account, that which was most
important was not merely believing that Christ was present in
the bread and wine, but recognizing and acknowledging,
through actions of care and concern, Christ's presence in the
Body—the members of the worshipping community. The
focus was not on the bread and the cup, but on the community and its lifestyle.

With the passing of the next few centuries, the celebration of the eucharist became increasingly standardized. When
the unity of the Church became a key issue, efforts were made
to regulate the celebration of the eucharist under the bishops'
authority. Gradually the fellowship meal described by Paul
disappeared and was replaced by a symbolic, ritual meal. The
basic pattern of eucharistic worship emerged during this time:
an offering of bread and wine, prayers of thanksgiving, breaking of bread and reception by all present. By the sixth century,
". . . Christian eucharistic worship [had] evolved from a com-
paratively brief and simple ritual meal into a richly elaborate
ceremonial liturgy."[2] The overall concern during this period
was, therefore, with the development and regulation of the celebration of the eucharist.

By the Middle Ages, an almost complete shift in emphasis was taking place. Once the pattern for worship had been
standardized, attention was turned to doctrinal matters. The
introduction of Aristotle into Western thinking lent new
thought forms and a new vocabulary to theology. This, coupled with the fact that certain theologians were beginning to
debate and reject the Church's traditional understanding of the
eucharist, forced the Church to renew steps to develop, clarify
and illuminate its own understanding of eucharistic doctrine.
The center of attention was no longer the liturgical action but
rather the doctrines of the real presence of Christ and the sacrifice of Christ in the Mass. Of primary importance, therefore,
were issues dealing with the eucharistic bread and wine: how

were the bread and wine changed into Christ's body and blood, and at what point did the sacrifice take place?

This concern with defining and clarifying the doctrine of the eucharist reached a veritable zenith during the Scholastic period of the 13th and 14th centuries. During these years, theologians struggled to find a metaphysical explanation that would make traditional faith in the real presence more intelligible. In so doing, many were caught up in exploring the means, manner and duration of Christ's presence in the eucharistic species. At times, however, this deep concern with the eucharistic bread and wine bordered on the ludicrous. Legalistic details concerning Christ's presence in the eucharist often appeared to overwhelm the meaning behind that presence. A classic example of this can be found in the *Summa Theologiae* of St. Thomas Aquinas. In regard to the reverence due the real presence of Christ in the elements, the question arose:

> It sometimes happens that a fly or spider or some venomous creature falls into the chalice after consecration [or that] by the priest's carelessness the blood of Christ is spilt, or that he vomits the sacrament received, or else that the consecrated hosts are kept so long that they decay or are nibbled by mice . . .

Thomas' answer gives witness to the fact that such problems were indeed a consideration: "If anything of the sort happens after consecration, the insect ought to be cautiously caught, thoroughly washed, and burnt, and the ablutions and ashes together poured into the piscina." In the case of the host partially destroyed by mold or mice, moreover, not only must the priest do penance for his neglect, but "whenever the species are found to be entire, they must be reverently kept or consumed, because so long as they be entire the body of Christ is there."[3]

Corresponding to this emphasis on doctrinal matters of real presence and sacrifice was a change in the practice of eucharistic worship. The priest was of greatest importance since he was the only person able to consecrate the bread and wine and enact the sacrifice. Attention came to be focused on the altar, the bread and wine and the person of the priest, while the worshipping community faded into the passive role of onlookers. Moreover, the spread of Jansenism led to a distorted emphasis on the unworthiness of humanity. This, coupled with an overemphasis on the divinity of Christ in the bread and wine, led to a decline of those who would partake of the eucharist and an increase of the adoration of the host. Furthermore, the fact that the Mass was said in Latin (a language understood primarily only by the clergy) meant that most people could not participate actively. As a result, separate devotions based on the adoration of the sacred species flourished and replaced communal eucharistic worship. Indeed, this occurred to such an extent that often

> the main object of the lay[person] in coming to Mass was to see the consecrated wafer, and for many the climax came when the priest elevated it after the Consecration. A warning bell was rung beforehand to alert the faithful, many of whom would wander around town going from church to church just to be present at the elevation. Sometimes they would pay the priest a special stipend just to hold the host up higher and for a longer time, and some even engaged in lawsuits in order to get the best place for viewing the host. This attitude gave rise to various devotions that focused on the host. The entire town would come out on such feasts as Corpus Christi in June, when the priest would carry the host through the town encased in a glittering gold monstrance.[4]

Hence, the eucharist was no longer a community celebration, but a rite presided over by the clergy. Is it any wonder that the ritual lacked meaning for those who attended?

Up until the time of the Second Vatican Council, most Roman Catholics seemed content to continue in their role as passive spectators at the eucharistic celebration. Vatican II, however, proved to be an enormous catalyst for change. Active participation in the eucharistic celebration by *all* members of the worshipping community was strongly endorsed by Council members. In order for this participation to occur, much of the eucharistic liturgy was both refined and reformed.

> The altar was brought forward, and the priest now faced the congregation; instead of whispering the prayers in Latin, he now read them aloud in the language of

the people. Many of the old rites and ceremonies were discarded.[5]

In the years since Vatican II, however, it has become increasingly evident that changes which concentrate primarily on external liturgical practices are not enough. While such external changes are undeniably of great significance and pivotal for changing the perception of the eucharist, the problems which are encountered in eucharistic theology today are not those that a change in externals alone can solve. Mere liturgical reform is insufficient.

Moreover, the demand for active participation which was advocated during the Second Vatican Council has led many people to the understanding that they are in fact an integral part of the eucharistic celebration. For the first time in centuries, many Catholics have been instilled with a distinct sense of ownership of the eucharist. And, with this sense of ownership, a deep desire on the part of many Catholics to rediscover and clarify the meaning of the eucharist for their own lives has occurred. For them, the mere reiteration of traditional doctrine will no longer suffice.

Furthermore, it is only too clear that the celebration of the eucharist continues to be beset with problems which are both theological and pastoral in nature. For example, the doctrine of the eucharist is expressed in terms which are highly technical and objective. As a result, most Roman Catholics, not having been trained in Aristotelian thought, have little understanding of the true meaning behind the eucharist. Furthermore, the prevailing crisis in attendance at the Sunday liturgy is ample evidence that many Roman Catholics are finding the celebration of the eucharist meaningless and irrelevant to their everyday lives as Christians. Moreover, the shortage of ordained ministers to preside at eucharistic celebrations is becoming acute. Hence, more and more Catholics are forced to live without a weekly eucharistic celebration.

In response to these ongoing concerns, there have been a number of attempts over the last thirty years to address at least one aspect of the crisis that is occurring in eucharistic theology. Two in particular have made a tremendous impact. In the 1960's, theologian Edward Schillebeeckx endeavoured to take specific aspects of traditional eucharistic doctrine and reinterpret them in terms that would be more meaningful and understandable to contemporary Catholics. In recognition of the fact that most twentieth century people no longer think in Scholastic terms, Schillebeeckx has tried to make the shift away from the framework of Aristotelian concepts in which the doctrine of the eucharist was formerly couched, to one of interpersonal relationships and significance. More recently, certain liberation theologians such as Tissa Balasuriya and Leonardo Boff have ventured even further from doctrinal issues, delving into previously little emphasized aspects of the eucharist. From interpreting the eucharist primarily in terms of the doctrines of the real presence and the sacrifice of the Mass, these theologians have shifted their attention to an equally important dimension: the link between the eucharist, justice and liberation.

Undeniably, the possibilities and implications which result from these attempts at eucharistic renewal are having a tremendous impact on numerous related areas of Roman Catholic theology today. Most significant, however, are the repercussions that are occurring specifically *within* the realm of eucharistic theology itself. It is becoming increasingly apparent that for the eucharist to remain irrelevant to the daily lives of people is to rob it of the significance and transformative power which is its true nature. A cry is being uttered which cannot be silenced. The eucharist *must* be taken beyond the traditional context and made relevant and meaningful to those who participate in its celebration. Indeed, contemporary Roman Catholics will accept no less.

Chapter One

The Official Doctrine of the Eucharist

IN DEALING WITH ROMAN CATHOLIC EUCHARISTIC THEOLOGY, modern theologians have inherited a rich background of experience and knowledge on which to base their own work. While it is true that eucharistic theology has traditionally centered around two major doctrines—the real presence of Christ in the eucharist (including such allied dogmas as the totality, permanence and manner of presence) and the sacrifice of Christ in the Mass—the development of eucharistic doctrine has by no means remained static. Centuries upon centuries of controversies with opponents coupled with numerous internal clarifications by Roman Catholic theologians have all contributed to the understanding of the eucharist with which we are familiar at present. Today's official doctrine of the eucharist is but the culmination of years of refinement.

Berengar of Tours

One such contributing factor to the clarification of the official doctrine of the eucharist was the controversy that centered around the teaching of Berengar of Tours in the eleventh century. This is not to say, of course, that eucharistic theology had never, up until that time, been debated. To the contrary, the controversy begun by Paschasius Radbertus in the ninth century over the identification of the eucharistic body of Christ and his natural, earthly body is ample evidence that the conflict between advocates of a spiritual interpretation based on Augustine and those of a realistic interpretation based on Ambrose was a constant one.[1] It was, nonetheless, the Berengarian controversy that led the Church to officially clarify and state its own understanding of the real presence and the change involved.

1. The Point at Issue

The exact point of issue in the Berengarian controversy often seems debatable.[2] While it is clear that Berengar unquestionably denied the dogma of transubstantiation, there are divided opinions as to whether or not he also denied the central dogma of the real presence. Although Berengar's blatant denial of transubstantiation did seem to be tantamount to a denial of the real presence, there were some indications that Berengar did in fact believe in the real presence. In his one surviving work, *De Sacra Coena*, phrases such as "You have it for certain that I say that the bread and wine of the altar are indeed the Body and Blood of Christ after consecration" and "The bread and wine on the altar are converted by the consecration into the true Body and Blood of Christ" seem to suggest a profound belief in the real presence.[3] There were, however, only a remarkably few and isolated such passages in all of Berengar's teaching.

Further proof of Berengar's denial of the real presence rests in the fact that scholars, when dealing with Berengar's theology of the eucharist, delineate two distinct stages in the controversy.[4] The first, from 1048 to 1059, was focused mainly on the real presence. Although there was some inquiry into the fact of a change and how this came about, orthodox writers at this time were primarily concerned with establishing the fact of the real presence.[5] It was not until the second stage of the controversy, after the 1059 profession of faith was signed by Berengar, that the emphasis was shifted to the interpretation of the conversion which took place during consecration and the theory of transubstantiation. Since Berengar's contemporaries were concerned with defending the doctrine of the real presence up until 1059, it seems obvious that they felt that his teachings advocated its denial.

Moreover, proof of Berengar's denial of the real presence rests in the fact that the doctrine was not even necessary according to his understanding of the eucharist. In stating that all religious value was in the elements themselves, there was no need in Berengar's theology for the actual body of Christ to be present.[6]

Finally, if Berengar had only been denying the theory of transubstantiation (which was not yet official church doctrine), something could have been worked out.

> Berengar was too acute a thinker to fail to perceive that if the only point at issue between himself and the authorities of the Church was his contention that the substance of the bread and wine remained, an effective compromise was possible at that date, when the doctrine of Transubstantiation was not so unreservedly demanded by the Church as at a later era.[7]

Hence, although it is undeniable that the majority of Berengar's efforts were directed to a more detailed criticism of transubstantiation, it is evident that Berengar was in fact also denying the real presence of Christ.

2. Berengar's Eucharistic Theology

From the beginning, Berengar consistently attacked the identification of Christ's physical body with the eucharistic body. That he denied a physical presence is incontrovertible: there was *no* physical change whatsoever in the elements of bread and wine after consecration. Nor did he believe there to be a substantial change. Not only was the substance of Christ *not* contained in the eucharistic species, but the substance of bread and wine remained. Instead, the fundamental principle of Berengar's conception of the eucharist was a dynamic symbolism which emphasized the effectiveness of the consecrated elements for the worthy recipient: "consecration surrounds the elements, for those who have faith and understanding, with the religious value of the body and blood of Christ."[8] Consecration, Berengar asserted, did in fact have an effect on the bread and wine insofar as it added the invisible spiritual significance of the heavenly body of Christ to the elements. A conversion did take place, but the elements remained what they were and had no personal relation to the earthly or risen body of Christ.[9]

Furthermore, whereas the Church taught that Christ's body and blood were not dependant on the faith of the recipient, Berengar insisted that the spiritual significance of the elements was totally dependent upon the recipient who, through faith and understanding, recognized that the elements were spiritually the body and blood of Christ. At consecration, the bread and wine were given the virtue of possessing the effectiveness of Christ's body and blood, but this effectiveness was only available to the recipient with faith: "The eucharist is the body of Christ for the inner man only. It is not in itself an objective quantity."[10]

This was not, however, a mere memorialist interpretation which sought to explain the eucharist as a purely emotional recollection of a distant Christ in heaven. Berengar's theory "does not waive aside the spiritual Body and Blood of Christ with an assertion that the consecrated elements are a mere picture or representation of their spiritual counterpart."[11] To the contrary, Berengar's emphasis on the spiritual feeding by faith strongly suggests that he did in fact maintain a doctrine of spiritual as opposed to corporeal presence. The consecrated elements, while not actually containing the body of Christ, were in fact symbolic of that body insofar as they exerted its significance to the faithful recipient. Berengar "insists that communion is efficacious and that, while the bread and the wine continue existing, they become a "sacrament"—that is, a 'sign' of the body of the Lord which is in heaven."[12]

Berengar, therefore, did in fact admit that insofar as the consecrated elements were given an added spiritual significance, a change did take place during consecration. That which he resolutely denied and emphatically rejected, however, was any notion of a *substantial* conversion of the bread and wine into the body and blood of Christ. This to Berengar was ludicrous: "the opinion of Paschasius and Lanfranc that the substance of bread and wine does not remain on the altar after consecration is madness."[13] The bread and wine were given a new religious value, but they did not cease to exist. The term "conversion" referred to the new religious significance rather than the metabolic change of the bread and wine. This was, of course, tantamount to a rejection of the Church's as yet undefined dogma of transubstantiation. Hence, "the fundamental difference between Berengar and his opponents over the real presence lay in the interpretation of the 'conversion' which took place through the consecration of the bread and wine."[14]

The grounds on which Berengar based his rejection were numerous. His first and leading idea was to introduce reason into Church doctrine. Accordingly, if one said that a substantial change took place at the consecration and yet still insisted that the bread and wine were the true body and blood of Christ, then the bread and wine must still exist or the proposition would be false.[15] Along the same lines, Berengar argued that a substantial conversion was contrary to reason insofar as an accident could not exist apart from its substance and a change of substance would necessarily mean a change of form. It would, therefore, be impossible for the substance of the bread and wine to be destroyed without its essential attributes also being destroyed.[16]

Moreover, Berengar rejected the idea of a substantial change on the grounds that it would be contrary to the laws of nature: "reason compels an admission that it is contrary to the law of nature that one thing can be changed into another without the breaking-up or annihilation of its original elements."[17] According to Berengar, if a material change had occurred, that change would have taken place in a substance which had not existed before. Given the fact that the body and blood of Christ had been in existence for ages, such a change was an impossibility. In addition, since Christ's body had existed in a state incapable of suffering and corruption since the Resurrection, that body could not be handled, broken and chewed as a substantial conversion would seem to imply.[18]

Berengar also repudiated transubstantiation on the simple grounds that it was contrary to the senses. After consecration, the bread was quite obviously still bread and the wine remained wine. No change in appearance was equated with no change in substance; if the bread and wine could be seen and touched, this meant they were there. Despite the seeming simplicity of this argument, it is ". . . the fundamental principle of the whole Berengarian criticism of the Catholic dogma of Transubstantiation. It is contrary to the evidence of the senses."[19]

3. Church's Response to Berengar's Eucharistic Theology

Berengar's denial of transubstantiation and of the real presence of Christ in the eucharistic species were, of course, viewed with great concern by the Church. Over a period of twenty years, Berengar was forced to take two oaths in an attempt to correct his thinking. While Berengar himself later repudiated both oaths, they were useful insofar as they were an attempt on the part of the Church to elaborate and clarify its own understanding of the eucharist.

Oath of 1059

Durand of Troarn. In formulating the oath of 1059, there were a number of theologians whose thought significantly influenced the eucharistic theology contained within the oath itself. One of these was Durand of Troarn. The uniqueness of Durand's thought lies in the fact that he outlined a distinct separation between two aspects of the eucharist: the outward appearance and the inner reality. "It is," McDonald maintains, "a new step in the attempt to define the difference between the eucharistic species and their spiritual significance."[20]

In regard to the spiritual significance, Durand asserted that while the eucharist was in some sense symbolical, it nonetheless possessed a real and true content. Although what the recipient received was a symbol of body or blood, it was still, through similitude, the real body and blood of Christ. The inner reality of the eucharist, then, was the true and substantial body and blood which was made available through the Incarnation:

> Although something different appears to human eyes, although as a type it is not denied that it usefully signifies something different, the sacramental element is actually nothing else substantially than the true flesh and blood of Christ.[21]

Although some difficulties were inherent in Durand's thought, his biggest contribution to eucharistic theology was his conception of the eucharistic presence as a substantial presence, probably the earliest use of the term *substantialiter.*[22] According to Durand, it was upon consecration that the substance of the body of Christ—flesh, blood, divinity and humanity—became present to the recipient. Since this substantial presence was brought about by an invisible change in the nature (rather than the form) of the elements, the real body of Christ remained invisible. Hence, included in Durand's defense of the real presence was an implicit theory of transubstantiation.

Bishop Humbert. Despite Durand's use of the term "substance," Bishop Humbert, who was in large part responsible for the wording of the confession of 1059, never used the term.[23] The sacramental body, in this early formula, was described as being "the true body and blood of our Lord Jesus Christ, and perceptibly not only in the Sacrament, but in reality, are touched and broken by the hands of the priest and ground by the teeth of the faithful."[24] No mention was made of the substance of Christ's body and blood. Neither did Humbert explain the change; he simply asserted that the bread and wine after consecration were the true body and blood, with no explanation as to how this occurred.

Oath of 1079

In spite of the fact that Berengar was forced to read the grossly realistic oath of 1059, never was he called on to make a written statement of consent to it. Soon after, then, he recanted what he had read in the oath and continued to further develop his own ideas.

Lanfranc. One of Berengar's major opponents during this time was Lanfranc, Archbishop of Canterbury, whose greatest contribution to the clarification of eucharistic theology was his theory of the eucharistic change. This change, as Lanfranc understood it, was a transformation in the essence of the elements:

> The bread and wine are changed in nature essentially. In their interior nature they are changed into those things which they were not before. They do not remain in their original essence.[25]

The eucharistic body of Christ, according to Lanfranc, did not exist before the consecration, but came into being as a result of it. It was the same body of Christ *in essence* as the historical body received by the Virgin and as the same glorified body which now existed in heaven. The appearance of it, however, was masked by the bread and wine. Qualities of bread and wine such as appearance, flavor and smell were retained as a visible cover for the body and blood of Christ. While this was not yet a complex theory of substance and accidents, it was nonetheless the basis for the establishment of the theory of transubstantiation.[26]

Lanfranc's theory of change had certain inherent weaknesses as well as strengths. Most significant was Lanfranc's claim that the bread and wine were themselves symbolic, not of the body and blood of Christ, but of the bread and wine that formerly existed before they were transformed into the essence of the body of Christ. At the same time, however, he also asserted that the material bread fed the body. As Justo Gonzalez questions: "How can a bread that does not exist nourish a body?"[27] Moreover, in spite of his assertion that the eucharistic body was identical with the historical body of Christ, Lanfranc still had to admit that the two were not entirely the same. The declaration that the eucharistic body (unlike Christ's historical body) did not exist before consecration seems to be in direct conflict with the assertion that the two are identical.

Part of Lanfranc's theory of change was his insistence on the *mystery* of the change involved. As a result of the attempts to assert the real presence throughout the time of the controversy, many crude, grossly physical terms had been used. The oath of 1059 in which Christ's body is said to be "ground by the teeth" is a prime example. By emphasizing the mystery of the change, Lanfranc was able to overcome some of the physical implications of his theory on the change of essence.

In addition, Lanfranc argued that faith was preferable to reason when attempting to interpret the change and content of the eucharist; belief in the real body of Christ was an exercise of faith. Hence, he wrote: "Rather do we believe that which we do not see, that faith may exist, for it cannot exist if what is to be believed can be perceived by the corporal senses."[28] This is not to say, however, that Lanfranc, like Berengar, believed that the presence of Christ was conditional on the perception and faith of the recipient. Rather, what was most important was *what* one received and not *how* one received. For Lanfranc, the real presence was an objective presence, independent of the subjective perception of the recipient.

Guitmond of Aversa. Another of Berengar's opponents who most influenced the wording of the 1079 confession of faith was Guitmond of Aversa.[29] Guitmond first refined the doctrine of the real presence by maintaining that while the historical body of Christ was in fact present, the eucharistic presence was nonetheless *sacramental* in nature. The eucharistic body, he claimed, had neither the appearance or the form of the historical body; although the bread was changed into the substantial body of Christ, this did not involve a change into actual flesh.[30]

Guitmond's greatest contribution to orthodox eucharistic theology was his assertion that the bread and wine were *substantially* changed into the body and blood of Christ. This "realism is such that he claims that the consecrated bread does not physically nourish the person who eats it."[31] That which was received and eaten in the eucharist, Guitmond insisted, was the true body in its substance; the whole substance of bread no longer existed.

Guitmond's use of the term "substance" was a major breakthrough both in safeguarding the belief in the real presence and in forcing Berengar to affirm his opponents' interpretation of the eucharistic change. The confession of 1079 thus reads:

> . . . the bread and wine which are placed on the altar are substantially changed into the true and proper and living flesh and blood of Jesus Christ, our Lord, and that after consecration it is the true body of Christ which was born of the Virgin and which, offered for the salvation of the world, was suspended on the Cross, and which sitteth at the right hand of the Father and the true blood of Christ, which was poured out from his side . . .[32]

The use of "substance" was an affirmation both of the real presence of Christ in the eucharist and of the identification of the historical body of Christ with the eucharistic body.

At the same time, Guitmond insisted that the eucharistic body was not capable of corruption or dissolution. Although it may have *seemed* that the body was broken and ground, this breaking and grinding only happened in actual fact to the elements. That which appeared to be destroyed were the accidents of the bread and wine. These accidents, however, existed without their substance since the substance of bread and wine had been replaced by the substance of Christ's body and blood.[33] While many difficulties are inherent in such an explanation, the important result of it was that the term "accidents" had become the corollary of "substance." Hence, "the way was prepared for the definitive statement of the doctrine of the real presence, which took the form of the dogma of transubstantiation."[34]

4. Results of the Controversy

As a result of the Berengarian controversy, substance and accidents became part of the standard vocabulary used by the Church to explain the process of the eucharistic change. In addition to contributing to the formulation of transubstantiation, the controversy "began the philosophic grounding of orthodox eucharistic teaching."[35]

In addition, the issue of the use of reason in theology was pushed to the forefront of the theological debate as a result of the Berengarian controversy. Berengar's main arguments against the real presence and transubstantiation were based on reason. As a result, he was often severely criticized for his lack of respect for authority. And yet, his opponents often used reason as a basis for their arguments as well. Hence, without solving the issue, the Berengarian conflict certainly brought it into the open for debate.

Most importantly, the Berengarian controversy inevitably was a factor that helped to clarify and unite the Church's teaching on eucharistic theology. Had the conflict not arisen, the Church would not have explored its own understanding of the eucharist to such a degree, nor would they have been forced to clarify and expound that understanding as an official dogmatic statement.

Thomas Aquinas' Eucharistic Theology

By the thirteenth century, the notion that faith and reason were ultimately compatible had become more widely accepted. More and more frequently, theologians were agreeing on the power of reason in reaching a deeper understanding of the Christian dogmas. The Scholastics, in particular, sought to create a synthesis between Aristotelian categories of thought and the Christian doctrinal system. The *Summa Theologiae* of Thomas Aquinas is one such example of the systematic effort to use reason in theology.[36]

Thomas' *Summa Theologiae* was written in the most comprehensive manner possible: "every important question of theology is treated from every angle conceivable in his day."[37] It was made up of ninety "articles" and covered a span of doctrinal issues which ranged from the existence and nature of God to the world order, from fear, anger and sin to grace and the sacraments. Of these ninety articles, eleven dealt specifically with the doctrine of the eucharist. Again, as in centuries past, the two major issues which were examined in this exposition on the eucharist were the sacrifice of the mass and the real presence. These two factors, Thomas contended, were what made the eucharist distinct and unique from the other sacraments.

While the majority of Thomas' treatise on the eucharist was devoted to a systematic, detailed exposition of the real presence—"In the other sacraments we have not got Christ himself really as we have in this sacrament."[38]—the sacrifice of the Mass was also examined in some detail: "This sacrament adds this to the other sacraments, the character of being a sacrifice."[39] While the explanation of the sacrificial aspect of the eucharist was considerably less than that of the real presence, this can perhaps be explained by the fact that a doctrine of sacrifice in many ways presupposed a belief in the real presence. Hence, as J. de Baciocchi explains: "On ne peut avoir la réalité de l'acte de donner sans avoir la réalité de l'être donné."[40]

1. The Doctrine of the Real Presence

For Thomas, the fact of the real presence was certain. In regard to those who argued that Christ's body and blood were only symbolically present in the eucharist, Thomas declared that such a position was heretical. He affirmed that it was right "that it should contain Christ himself who suffered for us, and contain him, not merely as by a sign or figure, but in actual reality as well."[41] This is to say, as he asserted in III, 73, 1 ad 3, that the eucharist contains something that is sacred *absolutely*—Christ himself—whereas the other sacraments contain something sacred not absolutely, but in relation to their power to justify. In the eucharist the distinctive source of grace was Christ's real presence in the bread and wine through which the recipient was united to God.

The presence of Christ in the eucharist was explained by Thomas in terms of transubstantiation: "The complete substance of the bread is converted into the complete substance of

Christ's body, and the complete substance of the wine into the complete substance of Christ's blood."[42]   At the moment of consecration, the words "This is my body . . . This is my blood," spoken by the validly ordained priest over the bread and wine transformed them into the substance of Christ's body and blood. This total conversion of the substance of the bread and the wine was, according to Thomas, the *only* way to render Christ present in the eucharist.[43]

In contrast to the other sacraments, the eucharist was fully established as soon as the words of institution were spoken over the elements of bread and wine. While it was the pouring of the water (and not the blessing of the water) which constituted baptism, the eucharist was accomplished as a result of consecration. Hence, Thomas wrote: "However, there is this difference, for other sacraments are accomplished in the application of their matter and are thus achieved in being received, but this sacrament is achieved in the consecration of the matter."[44]

By no means did Thomas understand this consecration as a magical act performed by the priest. Rather, when the priest uttered the words, he was acting as an instrument through which Christ spoke. Thus, "the priest consecrates this sacrament, not by his own power, but as Christ's minister in whose person he acts."[45] This transformation, moreover, was a result of divine power. In III, 75, 4, for example, Thomas declared: "This conversion, however, is not like any natural change, but it is entirely beyond the powers of nature and is brought about purely by God's action."

Thomas further contended that, after consecration, the substance of bread and wine no longer remained in the sacrament; they had not disappeared nor been annihilated, but had been transformed into the body and blood of Christ. The change which occurred, therefore, was an ontological change of substance.[46] This is not to say, of course, that the person who received the eucharist could actually see Christ's flesh and blood. Instead, as Thomas explained, God had arranged that while the substance of the bread and wine were changed, the accidents remained the same. What the person saw was not Christ's human appearance, but the bread and wine:

> Divine providence very wisely arranged for this. First of all, men have not the custom of eating human flesh and drinking human blood; indeed, the thought revolts them. . . Secondly, lest the sacrament should be an object of contempt for unbelievers, if we were to eat our Lord under his human appearance.[47]

Furthermore, Thomas insisted that Christ's body and blood were not subject to change after consecration. The actual body of Christ was *not* chewed and broken by the recipient:

> It remains then that the fraction takes place in the dimensive quantity of the bread, where all the other accidents find their subject. And just as the sacramental species are the sign of the real body of Christ, so the fraction of these species is the sign of our Lord's passion which he endured in his actual body.[48]

With this explanation, then, the grossly realistic interpretation of the real presence which had arisen during the Berengarian controversy was avoided.

The mode of Christ's presence in the sacrament was a spiritual, non-visible and non-physical one according to Thomas. Christ's body was *not* in the sacrament in its natural appearance or form. Nor was it in the sacrament in the same way that a body was in a place, with its dimensions corresponding to the dimensions of the place which contained it. Rather, "wherever this sacrament is celebrated he is present in an invisible way under sacramental appearance . . . Christ's body is here in a special way that is proper to this sacrament."[49] Hence, the mode of Christ's presence in the eucharist was a sacramental one.

It was at this point, Thomas affirmed, that the need for faith arose. Since Christ's presence was an invisible one, it would be impossible for a person to know by virtue of the senses that Christ's body and blood were truly present. It was the person's faith, then, which was given by God, that had to accept what could not be seen or sensed. "Now faith," Thomas wrote, "has to do with unseen realities, and just as he offers his divinity to our acceptance as something that we do not see, so in this sacrament he offers his very flesh to us in like manner."[50] Because Christ had testified, by means of the words with which he instituted the eucharist, that he would be truly present in the sacrament, the person was to believe this to be true. Hence, the eucharist was itself an object of faith.

Due to Christ's real presence in the bread and wine, the eucharist was for Thomas quite obviously a source of grace. Thomas was adamant, however, that this not be understood in terms of a mechanistic bestowal of grace. In order to avoid such a misunderstanding, Thomas insisted on maintaining a distinction between sacramental and spiritual eating which seemed to accurately emphasize the need for faith and a correct disposition on the part of the recipient. Sacramental eating, Thomas declared, was when the sacrament was received without the reception of the resultant grace.[51] For example, in the case of the person who was in the state of mortal sin (and cognizant of the fact) or even in the case of the person who did not have a correct spiritual disposition, reception of the sacrament did not mean automatic appropriation of its grace. This is not to say that the person did not actually receive Christ's body and blood; if the bread and wine had been properly consecrated, they were and remained Christ's body and blood.[52] However, not only did the unworthy recipient *not* receive the grace contained in the eucharist, but, if in a state of mortal sin, he earned condemnation.[53] Sacramental eating, then, was limited to the physical act of receiving the eucharist.

Spiritual eating, on the other hand, included sacramental eating but added to it insofar as both the body and blood of Christ and the resultant grace were received. Thomas explained:

> Since then the embryonic and the full-grown are contrasted, so the sacramental eating, in which the sacrament is received without its effect, is contrasted with the spiritual eating in which is received the sacramental effect whereby a person is spiritually joined to Christ in faith and charity.[54]

It is especially interesting to note that while Thomas maintained that the actual reception of the eucharist did confer grace more fully, it was nonetheless possible to receive grace without it. Even if the sacrament could not be eaten sacramentally, it could still be received spiritually if the desire for it was present.[55]

According to Thomas, the greatest grace resulting from spiritual eating of the eucharist was the forgiveness of sins. There were, however, many distinctions. For example, insofar as a person was conscious of mortal sin, that person could not receive the forgiveness resultant of the eucharist. Nonetheless, if a person was in a state of mortal sin, but was not cognizant of the fact, the sin would be forgiven upon reception of (or even as a result of the desire to receive) the eucharist. Venial sins, on the other hand, could always be forgiven. For Thomas, then, the eucharist was the sacrament of forgiveness: "The power is there of forgiving any sin whatever from Christ's Passion, who is the font and cause of our being forgiven."[56]

In addition, Thomas affirmed that the eucharist had a preservative effect against future sin. As spiritual food for the soul, the eucharist built up the strength by which the recipient could ward off the future attacks of sin: "By joining him to Christ through grace [the eucharist] strengthens his spiritual life, as spiritual food and spiritual medicine."[57] For Thomas, the real presence of Christ in the eucharistic species was a source of spiritual nourishment for those who received it. As such, he concluded, "the eucharist is the summit of the spiritual life and all the sacraments are ordered to it."[58]

2. The Sacrifice of the Mass

Although Thomas placed great emphasis on his exposition of the real presence of Christ in the eucharist, he also treated at some length the doctrine of the sacrifice of the Mass. His treatment of this doctrine is, however, quite brief as compared with that of the doctrine of the real presence. Perhaps the greatest reason for this, as Francis Clarke suggests, is "that no significant controversies had arisen on that question, whereas the controversies about the real presence had provided a fertile field for discussion."[59] Thomas' exposition of the sacrifice of the Mass was, then, for the most part a reiteration of the traditional understanding of the Mass as sacrifice, with little elaboration and few additions.

The essence of the eucharistic sacrifice, according to Thomas, was the sacrifice of Christ. At one point, quoting Augustine, Thomas affirmed: "Once Christ was sacrificed in his very self, yet daily he is sacrificed in the Mass" and at another point in the same article, declared that "it is peculiar to this sacrament that in its celebration Christ is the sacrifice."[60]

The fact that Christ was indeed present in the eucharist under the species of bread and wine was for Thomas a certainty. Logically, then, since Christ was present in this way during the representation of His Passion that occurred in the Mass, it must necessarily be Christ himself who was sacrificed: "the eucharist is the perfect sacrament of Our Lord's Passion, because it contains Christ himself who endured it."[61]

It was, Thomas contended, the double consecration of the bread and wine which in fact effected the re-presentation of the Passion of Christ: "Thomas located the sacrifice of the Mass not in an offering of the body and blood of Christ subsequent to the consecration, but in the consecration of the elements themselves."[62] Hence, in affirming that both Christ's body and blood were in fact present under each species, Thomas concluded that: "there is a point in having the two species. First of all, this serves to represent Christ's passion, in which his blood was separated from his body."[63] That which accomplished the sacrifice, therefore, was the actual consecration of bread and wine which made them into the body and blood of Christ.

The real presence of Christ in the eucharist was affirmed by Thomas as proof that Christ was in fact sacrificed in the Mass. In other words, this assertion meant that the sacrifice of the Mass was the *same* sacrifice as that of Calvary insofar as the victim of the sacrifice was the same—Christ.[64] And yet, while emphasizing the identity of the two, Thomas necessarily maintained that Christ was present as victim in the sacrifice of the Mass under the sacramental species and in an unbloody manner: "But the body of Christ is not eaten as under its natural form, but as under the sacramental species."[65]

Furthermore, not only was the victim the same in both the sacrifice of the cross and the sacrifice of the Mass, but so also, according to Thomas, was the priest, again albeit in a sacramental way. While he did in fact give great importance to the power of the priest who consecrated the bread and wine and who communicated in the person of all present, Thomas was nonetheless most emphatic in his assertion that the priest was not acting in his own person, but in the person of Christ. "The priest," he explained, "consecrates this sacrament, not by his own power, but as Christ's minister in whose person he acts."[66] The priest, therefore, was in essence Christ himself.

In order to explain why the celebration of the eucharist was called the sacrifice of Christ, Thomas further expanded on the description of the Mass as the memorial and re-presentation of Christ's sacrifice on Calvary. Quoting Augustine, he explained:

> As Augustine writes, Images are called by the names of the things of which they are images, thus looking at a picture or fresco we say, That is Cicero, or, That is Sallust. Now, as we have said, the celebration of this sacrament is a definite image representing Christ's passion, which is his true sacrifice.[67]

As a memorial of Christ's Passion, the eucharist was to commemorate the Passion that happened in the past, as Christ himself requested at the Last Supper: "This sacrament was instituted at the Lord's Supper that it might in the future be a memorial of the Passion when that had been accomplished."[68]

More importantly, however, was the notion of the Mass as *the* re-presentation of Christ's Passion. Thomas' concept of a re-presentative image in no way meant a mere mental recollection of the unique sacrifice of Calvary on the part of the worshippers. As J. de Baciocchi attests, Thomas did not use the term 're-presentation' in the sense "qui suggère une simple évocation mentale sans présence effective de l'objet ou de l'évenement."[69] Rather, Thomas' use of the term could better be expressed as a re-presentation wherein the sacrifice of the mass once again made present the sacrifice of Calvary. In his own words: "[The eucharist] has the nature of a sacrifice inasmuch as it makes present Christ's Passion."[70] The sacrifice of the Mass was not, therefore, a different sacrifice from that of Calvary but a re-presentation of it; the sacrifice of the Mass *is*

Christ's sacrifice of the Cross offered in a sacramental manner.

There were, Thomas insisted, various ways in which the eucharist re-presented the Passion. The eucharist, he noted, was the only sacrament that was both received and offered, and insofar as it was offered, it had the nature of a sacrifice.[71] At still another point, Thomas declared that the host was broken during Mass in order to signify the breaking of Christ's body during his Passion.[72] As well, in III, 76, 2 ad 1, Thomas explained that the fact that the eucharist consisted of two species signified the Passion in which Christ's blood was separated from his body. Likewise, at another point, he affirmed that: "the blood consecrated separately from the body gives us a more vivid representation of Christ's Passion."[73] Hence, further proof is shown of Thomas' assertion that it was by means of the double consecration that the Passion of Christ was most effectively re-presented.

Finally, intricately linked with the affirmation of the Mass as the re-presentation of Christ's Passion was Thomas' assertion that the eucharist was the sacrifice of Christ insofar as it carried on and applied the effects of that Passion which it re-presented. The forgiveness of sins won on the cross was, in the Mass, applied to each individual. Since it was Christ's Passion that was re-presented, "accordingly the effect his Passion wrought in the world the sacrament works in a man."[74] The sacrifice of the Mass, therefore, was one with the sacrifice of Calvary.

Council of Trent

In 1520, three years after the Ninety Five Theses were nailed to the church door in Wittenberg, Martin Luther wrote *The Babylonian Captivity of the Church,* a treatise which sharply attacked many central tenets of the Roman Catholic doctrine of the eucharist. The debate escalated and took on new dimensions as Reformer after Reformer called into question traditional Catholic eucharistic doctrine. Continual controversies and disputes with people such as Luther, Zwingli and Carl-stadt provided the stimulus needed for the Church to call the Council of Trent in 1545. Once again, dissention over and opposition to eucharistic doctrines were forcing the Church to outline and give official status to its own understanding of the eucharist.

The importance of the clarification of the doctrine of the eucharist for the participants at the Council of Trent was obvious: more time and thought were devoted to the exposition on the eucharist than to all the other sacraments combined. This exposition was, however, in no way meant to be a complete analysis of eucharistic doctrine. Rather, it was a reaction against the doctrine as set out by the Reformers:

> The Fathers had no intention of giving an exhaustive exposition of all the aspects of sacramental doctrine; they intended that the decrees constitute only the necessary minimum, in opposition and contrast to the prevailing heresies.[75]

As a result, the decrees of the Council were polemical in tone.

While it is true that many practical issues such as communion under both species and the use of the vernacular were dealt with by the Council Fathers, the two main doctrinal issues were, once again, the real presence of Christ in the eucharist and the sacrifice of the Mass. Furthermore, in light of the fact that the Council was in many ways a response to the Reformers, only those features of the real presence and the sacrifice of the mass which had been disputed were treated in great depth in the decrees. Little mention was made of those issues on which the Reformers and the Roman Catholic Church were in agreement.

1. The Doctrine of the Real Presence

There are two essential affirmations in Trent's *Decree on the Most Holy Eucharist*: that of a distinct, real and sacramental presence of Christ in the eucharist and that of the change of the bread and wine into the body and blood of Christ which this real presence demanded.[76] According to most scholars, the basic concern of this thirteenth session of Trent was to clarify exactly *what* was contained in the eucharist: "The speci-fication of that content was the most important issue in the first stage of the conciliar discussions, for on this issue most of the others depended."[77] This concern, then, led to both the af-firmation of the doctrine of the real presence of Christ as well as the affirmation of the aptness of the dogma of transubstan-tiation that was the means used to express the real presence.

Affirmation of the Real Presence of Christ in the Eucharist[78]

The first doctrinal issue which was dealt with at Trent was certain Reformers' assertions that the body and blood of Christ were present in the eucharist only as in a sign or figure. Zwingli and Carlstadt (among others) had denied the real presence and insisted instead upon a symbolic interpretation of the words of institution.[79] The result of such an interpreta-tion was that the eucharist was seen as a meal of remembrance only. According to these Reformers, then, the whole point of the eucharist was to remember Christ's saving death and, by faith, lift oneself to heaven to commune with Christ there.

In response to this denial of the real presence, the Coun-cil Fathers re-affirmed the actual reality of Christ's presence in the eucharist by issuing the following canon:

> If anyone denies that in the sacrament of the most holy Eucharist there are truly, really, and substantially con-tained the body and blood together with the soul and divinity of our Lord Jesus Christ, and therefore the whole Christ, but shall say that He is in it as by a sign or figure, or force, let him be anathema.[80]

That which was present in the eucharist was Christ in his en-tirety—body, blood, soul and divinity. The change which took place in the elements, therefore, was necessarily a radical change of being.

How this real presence was possible was explained by the Fathers in terms of concomitance. That is, Christ's body and blood were present in the sacrament by obvious virtue of the words of institution. By virtue of concomitance—that is, by virtue of the fact that all parts of Christ are united—Christ's divinity and soul were also present. Hence, Chapter Three of the *Decree* stated: "by force of that natural concomitance by which the parts of Christ the Lord . . . are mutually united, the divinity also because of that admirable hypostatic union with His body and soul."[81] Carrying this even a step further, the Fathers asserted that Christ was wholly and entirely present under each species and each part of each species. Christ's body and blood, soul and divinity were therefore present in their entirety under the species of the bread alone or the wine alone, as well as under each fragment or drop of the bread and wine. Hence, Chapter Three concluded: "For Christ whole and entire exists under the species of bread and under any part whatsoever of that species, likewise the whole Christ is present under the species of wine and under its parts."[82] Communion under one species alone was therefore entirely valid.

The manner in which Christ was present in the sacrament was explained in the *Decree* in the following terms: "truly," "really," "substantially" and "contained under the species." The word "truly" expressed the belief that the real presence was in accord with the words of Christ, who clearly stated, "This is my body." "Really" was used to discredit the belief that Christ was present only in a figurative manner. The term "substantially" emphasized the fact that that which was contained was Christ's very being—human and divine. "Contained under the species," finally, signified that Christ's presence was not a spatial presence, but a sacramental one which was not in the least contradictory to His presence at the right hand of the Father.[83]

Like Thomas, the Council members further reaffirmed the real presence of Christ in the eucharist by maintaining the excellence of the eucharist over the other sacraments. In Chapter Three, it was declared that "this excellent and peculiar thing is found in it, that the other sacraments first have the power of sanctifying, when one uses them, but in the Eucharist there is the Author of sanctity Himself before it is used."[84] This was to say that Christ was bodily present in the eucharist upon consecration. It was, therefore, an objective presence which was not dependent upon either its use or its reception. Contrary to the Reformers' insistence on the importance of faith in the reception of the eucharist, the Council Fathers adamantly maintained that Christ was present in the eucharist regardless of the recipient's faith.

The Council's insistence on the lasting presence or permanence of Christ in the eucharist re-emphasized the fact of the real presence. In Canon Four, for example, an anathema was pronounced on anyone who denied that Christ's body and blood were present "only in its use, while it is taken, not however before or after, and that in the hosts or consecrated particles, which are reserved or remain after communion."[85] Contrary to certain Reformers' opinions that Christ's body and blood were present only for the purpose of reception or communion, Chapter Five and Six of the *Decree* insisted on the appropriateness of the reservation of the sacrament both for veneration and to be taken to the sick. The affirmation of the reservation of the sacrament pointed to the permanence of Christ's presence therein.[86]

Transubstantiation

In addition to examining and safeguarding the Church's belief in the doctrine of the real presence, the Council of Trent also found it necessary to define the change of substance which was being used to affirm the real presence and which many of the Reformers were denying. Martin Luther, for example, while retaining the traditional doctrine of the real presence, denied both the complete conversion of substance and the separation of substance and accidents which were necessary factors in the dogma of transubstantiation. For Luther, the doctrine of the real presence should not have been dependent on transubstantiation. Transubstantiation, he argued, was merely an opinion rather than an article of faith and could, therefore, be held or not held with freedom.[87] Nonetheless, he did list transubstantiation alongside with the withholding of the cup from the laity and the sacrifice of the mass as one of the three captivities of the sacrament, calling it "a monstrous word and a monstrous idea."[88]

In response to the Reformers' denial of transubstantiation, the Council vehemently declared: "by the consecration of the bread and wine a conversion takes place of the whole substance of bread into the substance of the body of Christ our Lord, and of the whole substance of the wine into the substance of His blood."[89] This affirmation of a total conversion, as was further explained in Canon Two, necessarily implied first that the substance of bread and wine no longer existed after consecration and second, that only the species of bread and wine remained.[90] The whole substance of bread and wine were therefore converted into the whole substance of Christ's body and blood which were, nonetheless, contained under the remaining species of bread and wine.

Indeed, both the chapter and the canon which dealt with transubstantiation affirmed the appropriateness of the term itself. "This conversion," Chapter Four continued, "is appropriately and properly called transubstantiation by the Catholic Church."[91] The use of the term, as many scholars insist, was met by some opposition. Schillebeeckx, for example, explains that some of the Council Fathers expressed the concern that the Council should not use a term which had been introduced so recently into Roman Catholic eucharistic theology.[92] Jaroslav Pelikan, furthermore, explains that there was some hesitation about its use because of the reason it had first been used by the Church. Of one of the Council Fathers in particular, Pelikan explains:

> While he acknowledged that 'since the beginning of the church there has scarcely been a more general and universal' council than the Fourth Lateran, he had nevertheless come to the conclusion that the outside pressure of heresy rather than the inherent appropriateness of the term had been responsible for that council's adoption of transubstantiation.[93]

Despite this opposition, however, transubstantiation was defended as the legitimate tradition of the Church and was subsequently used by the Council as *the* manner of expressing the real presence of Christ in the eucharist. Perhaps the best explanation for this is the fact that the term itself had become, in Schillebeeckx' words, "a political banner of the orthodox faith, very suitably proclaiming in the sixteenth-century situation, the difference between the Reformers' and the Catholic view of the Eucharist."[94]

In spite of the philosophical implications of the term "transubstantiation," most scholars agree that the Council Fathers did not sanction one particular philosophical framework as a necessary part of the dogma of transubstantiation.[95] Thomas Ambrogi, for example, declares that "the dogmatic definition does not include the necessary identity of the dogma with its expression in an aristotelian-scholastic dialectic of substance and accidents."[96] With regards to the term "substance," many scholars agree that it was not intended to be understood in a precise philosophical sense, but was rather used in the ordinary sense. "Substance," then, was understood by the Council Fathers to mean the profound reality of a thing as distinct from its appearance.[97]

Furthermore, the word "accidents" did not appear at all in the official decree, but was replaced by the term "species" as the corollary of "substance." By not using the term "accidents," any suggestions of systematic philosophy were denied: "when the word 'substance' is deprived of its habitual partner (represented, in the technical language of the time, by the word 'accidents'), it is detached from the philosophical universe in which it normally moves."[98] Due to the disassociation of "substance" and "accidents," then, any implications that Aristotelian philosophy must necessarily be used to explain the change of substance of bread and wine into the body and blood of Christ were thereby avoided.

The major concern of the Council Fathers was *not* for the term itself or the philosophy implied, but for the affirmation of the profundity of the change which the term "transubstantiation" aptly suggested. This is to say that transubstantiation had become *the* official means by which the radical ontological change demanded by the real presence was expressed and safeguarded.[99]

2. The Doctrine of the Sacrifice of the Mass

Eleven years after the *Decree on the Most Holy Eucharist* was issued, another important document dealing with the eucharist was written: *The Doctrine on the Most Holy Sacrifice*. The issue of the sacrifice of the Mass was, once again, one that was greatly contested by many of the Reformers. Luther, for example, adamantly maintained that "as the greatest of all abominations I regard the mass when it is preached or sold as a sacrifice or good work."[100] Of significant importance is the fact that the exposition of the doctrine of the sacrifice of the

Mass had, with the exception of the work of Thomas Aquinas, not been very noteworthy up until the time of the Reformation. As John Hughes aptly explains:

> The Catholic apologists in the Reformation period were hampered by the fact that they had inherited no living theology of eucharistic sacrifice. For several centuries the theologians had concentrated their attention more and more on the question of the real presence.[101]

It was, therefore, the task of the Council Fathers to delineate as clearly as possible a theology of eucharistic sacrifice and to maintain that theology as official Roman Catholic teaching.

The main doctrinal point to be set forth by the Council was the affirmation that the eucharist was a true and proper sacrifice insofar as Christ himself was contained under the species of bread and wine: "If anyone says that in the mass a true and real sacrifice is not offered to God, or that the act of offering is nothing else than Christ being given to us to eat: let him be anathema."[102] The sacrifice of the Mass was to be understood as the sacrifice of Christ himself through the priest. That God desired this to be so was obvious to the Fathers: it was foretold through Malachi, prefigured in the sacrifice of the Old Testament, and affirmed by Paul.[103]

The priesthood, furthermore, was established by Christ especially for the purpose of offering this sacrifice: through them Christ would continue forever the sacrifice which he began at the Last Supper when he offered himself to the Father. At the Last Supper, Christ "offered to God the Father His own body and blood under the species of bread and wine, and under the symbols of those same things gave to the apostles (whom He then constituted priests of the New Testament)."[104]

Much attention was also given to the relationship between the sacrifice of the Cross and the sacrifice of the Mass. The Reformers' claim that the sacrifice of the Mass took away from or implied that something was missing from the sacrifice of the Cross, forced the Council Fathers to effectively describe and elaborate on the relation between the two.[105] The Fathers countered this attack by insisting that the sacrifice of the Mass did not cast blasphemy upon the sacrifice of the Cross precisely because the two sacrifices were the same. Insofar as "it is one and the same Victim, the same now offering by the ministry of priests as He who then offered Himself on the Cross," the sacrifice of the Mass is at one with that of the Cross.[106] The only difference between the two was the manner of offering. Through the priest, Christ did in fact offer Himself under the species of bread and wine, albeit in an unbloody manner. The difference, therefore, was that on the Cross Christ was immolated in a bloody manner; in the eucharist, he was immolated in an unbloody manner under the sacramental species.

The sacrifice of the Mass was believed by the Fathers to be a true sacrifice in and of itself. As Thomas Ambrogi clarifies, however, "the Mass is not an absolute sacrifice, but was instituted at the Last Supper as a relative sacrifice."[107] This is to say that the Mass was in itself a true sacrifice that was nonetheless related to the sacrifice of the Cross and a re-presentation of it. The Mass was more than a mere commemoration of the Cross (although it was that too); it was a re-presentation which made that once-for-all sacrifice present. Hence, in Chapter One it was declared that Christ left the Church a visible sacrifice, "whereby that bloody sacrifice once completed on the Cross might be represented."[108]

In addition, certain Reformers proposed that the Mass was only a commemoration of the sacrifice of Calvary or that the only sacrifice contained in the Mass was that of praise and thanksgiving. As a result, the Council Fathers were forced to go a step beyond the idea of the Mass as a re-presentation of the sacrifice of the Cross and forcefully assert that the sacrifice of the Mass was in fact a propitiatory sacrifice.[109] Through it, they insisted, the forgiveness of sin won on the Cross was applied to the individual person who approached the Mass with faith and repentance: "the fruits of that oblation (bloody, that is) are received most abundantly through this unbloody one."[110] And, not only was the forgiveness of sin applied to the repentant person, but so also the punishment and satisfaction for sin. Finally, according to the Council, the sacrifice of the Mass applied the merits of the Cross not only to those who received, but to all people, living and dead, for whom it was offered. It is important to note, however, that great emphasis was placed on the fact that the merits of the sacrifice of the Mass were solely a result of those won on the Cross. All efficacy of the Mass, therefore, was due to the sacrifice of the Cross and was in no way derogatory to that once-for-all sacrifice.[111]

Conclusion

For centuries, Roman Catholic theologians grappled with the Church's teaching on the eucharist. Dissention over the correct understanding of the sacrament forced the Church to clarify and unite its teaching and then to officially state its own position. As a result of the Berengarian controversy, for example, previously widely accepted concepts became official teaching. Aquinas' exposition of the eucharist gave a systematic and in depth presentation of the Catholic doctrines of the real presence and the sacrifice of the Mass, while the Council of Trent for the most part re-affirmed that traditional teaching in an official capacity.

From these centuries of debate, two major doctrinal pre-occupations stand out: the real presence of Christ in the eucharistic species and the sacrifice of the Mass.

With regards to the doctrine of the real presence, a certain objectivity gradually crept in. While Berengar insisted that without the faith of the recipient, Christ could not be present, Aquinas taught that although faith was in fact necessary for spiritual eating, Christ was present regardless of the individual's faith. In reaction to certain Reformers, Trent reaffirmed this by stating that Christ was bodily present in the Eucharist regardless of the faith of the believer and for as long as the species of bread and wine existed. Moreover, the objectivity of Christ's presence in the sacrament both before and after communion gave special status to the eucharist. Both Thomas and the Council of Trent affirmed that because Christ was present in the other sacraments only in their use, the eucharist alone was the summit of spiritual life. Hence, the centrality of the eucharist became increasingly evident during these centuries.

In addition, it was during these years that the theory of transubstantiation was recognized as *the* valid means of expressing the reality of Christ's presence in the bread and wine. While the term transubstantiation was not given official status until 1215 at the Fourth Lateran Council, it was undeniably as a result of the Berengarian controversy of the eleventh century that the term "substance" became associated with official eucharistic doctrine. The whole understanding of transubstantiation was further developed and expanded by Thomas. By 1551 at the Council of Trent, belief in a change of substance had become synonymous with belief in the real presence.

With regards to the doctrine of the sacrifice of the Mass, the belief that the Mass was a true, proper and propitiatory sacrifice was insisted upon by Roman Catholic theologians. However, the fact that the sacrifice of the Mass was reliant on the unique, all-sufficient sacrifice of the cross continued to be emphasized. The Mass was, therefore, related to the Cross insofar as it was a re-presentation of that sacrifice, a memorial of it, and most importantly, the application of the merits of that sacrifice.

This, then, is the official Roman Catholic doctrine of the eucharist which has been passed down through the centuries to the present day. Overall, one fact has remained evident. For Roman Catholics, the eucharist was not simply one of seven sacraments, but *foremost* among them. It was, and remains, central to the core of Roman Catholicism.

Discussion Questions

1. What are the two major doctrinal issues which have dominated Roman Catholic theology for centuries? Briefly describe the Catholic understanding of each.

2. Why was the Berengarian controversy significant in the development of the doctrine of the real presence?

3. How did Berengar's understanding of the change involved in the real presence differ from official teaching?

4. How did the oaths of 1059 and 1079 differ from one another?

5. What was the goal of Scholasticism?

6. Why did Thomas spend more time developing the doctrine of the real presence than the doctrine of the sacrifice of the Mass?

7. How did Thomas express the mode of Christ's presence?

8. What is the difference between sacramental and spiritual eating?

9. What did Thomas mean by "re-presentation"?

10. What was it, according to Thomas, which effected the sacrifice of Christ in the Mass?

11. In what ways did the sacrifice of the Mass differ from the sacrifice of the Cross?

12. What points of traditional Roman Catholic eucharistic doctrine did the Reformers call into question? How did the Council of Trent refute these denials?

13. Describe the Council's exploration of transubstantiation. Do you think Aristotelian philosophy was a necessary component of the dogma?

14. Why were the participants at Trent hampered when it came to defending the doctrine of the sacrifice of the Mass against the Reformers?

15. Describe the different understanding of the role that faith played in the eucharistic celebration in the theology of Berengar, Aquinas and the Council of Trent. Which is closest to your own understanding of the role of faith? Explain.

16. According to medieval eucharistic theology, what is it that makes the eucharist foremost among the sacraments? Is this still true today?

Chapter Two

Aggiornamento—Eucharistic Renewal at Vatican II

WITH LITTLE CHANGE, THE EUCHARISTIC DOCTRINE WHICH was developed in the Middle Ages and culminated at the Council of Trent is the understanding of the eucharist which has prevailed into the twentieth century. For the majority of Roman Catholics, these two doctrines of the real presence of Christ and the sacrifice of the Mass defined the *essence* of the eucharist. In the latter part of the twentieth century, however, certain astute theologians came to recognize that the majority of Catholics attended the eucharistic celebrations as passive spectators who had little understanding of the true meaning behind the eucharist. In many ways, the eucharist had lost its transforming meaning and was but a shell of what it was meant to be.

In recognition of this lack of meaning which the eucharist held for many people, the twentieth century liturgical movement in general and the *Constitution on the Sacred Liturgy* of

Vatican II in particular set out to restore that meaning. The culmination of many decades of work, the *Constitution on the Sacred Liturgy* promulgated in 1963 at the Second Vatican Council has as its primary goal the reform of the eucharistic liturgy. Reform, however, is not meant to be viewed in terms of revolution. Rather, the reform of the liturgy is to be understood as a revitalization of that which already exists:

> The reform of the liturgy cannot be a revolution. It must try to grasp the real meaning and the basic structure of the traditional rites and, making prudent use of existing deposits, build them on organically in the direction indicated by the pastoral needs of a living liturgy.[1]

Doctrinal issues centering around the real presence or sacrifice of the Mass, while important, are not central to the *Constitution*. What is important is that the ritual itself be made meaningful for the majority of Roman Catholic laypeople who attended the Sunday liturgies. Relevance is the key word for expressing that which is sought: reform of the liturgy must make the traditional rites meaningful and applicable for those who take part in them now.

Liturgical Movement

For decades before Vatican II, the liturgical reform movement had been a vital force in the Roman Catholic church; a force which promoted the active participation of all members of the church.[2] Starting as early as 1903 with Pope Pius X's decree on frequent communion, the whole idea of a liturgical reform gradually gained momentum until, in 1947, the call to reform was given official sanctioning: *Mediator Dei* was issued on November 20 of that year. In it, Pius XII ratified the liturgical movement of the previous decades and culminated his approval with the statement that "the Christian community is in duty bound to participate in the liturgical rites according to their station."[3] The entire aim of this reform was

. . . to make full meaning of the liturgy and the sacraments more manifest, thus assisting the faithful to enter into them more deliberately and more effectively and so benefit, not only *ex opere operato* (which does not vary), but also as much as possible *ex opere operantis* (which does vary enormously).[4]

Active participation was the hoped-for end result of the movement.

Despite the emphasis of the liturgical movement on participation, however, a theological and doctrinal grounding was still perceived as a necessary basis for reform. This is to say that, in order to participate, people must have some theological knowledge about that in which they are participating. In *Mediator Dei*, for example, the doctrine of the sacrifice of the Mass as set out by Trent was resolutely maintained: "the Church prolongs the priestly mission of Jesus Christ . . . in the first place at the altar, where constantly the sacrifice of the Cross is re-presented and, with a single difference in the manner of its offering, renewed."[5] Likewise, the real presence of Christ in the eucharist was also clearly taught in that same document: "Christ is present at the august sacrifice of the altar . . . above all under the eucharistic species."[6]

However, while keeping traditional doctrine as a basis, the emphasis of the liturgical movement was clearly focused for the most part on the practical, pastoral aspect of the liturgy. Such an emphasis can quite likely be attributed to the fact that the practical aspect (especially participation) had largely been neglected in previous centuries. By developing and asserting traditional eucharistic doctrine against prevailing heresies, many practical issues had been all but ignored.

Vatican II—Conciliar Eucharistic Theology

On 4 December 1963, the *Constitution on the Sacred Liturgy*—the first official document to come out of Vatican II—was promulgated. As a constitution, this document has a definite permanency to it: it is not meant to settle temporary questions but rather is a permanent Church law which must be adhered to. However, the document is presented not so much as a dogmatic statement but as a pastoral guideline which must nonetheless be carried out to the fullest possible extent.[7]

1. Renewal of the Liturgy

One of the key words which is often associated with the Second Vatican Council in general and Pope John XXIII in particular is *aggiornamento*—renewal. No where does this theme of renewal become more evident than in the *Constitution on the Sacred Liturgy*. From the very outset, it is apparent that the goal of the *Constitution* is in fact the renewal of the liturgy:

> It is the goal of this most sacred Council to intensify the daily growth of Catholics in Christian living; to make more responsive to the daily requirements of our times those Church observances which are open to adaptation; to nurture whatever can contribute to the unity of all who believe in Christ; and to strengthen those aspects of the Church which can help summon all of mankind into her embrace. Hence the Council has special reasons for judging it a duty to provide for the renewal and fostering of the liturgy.[8]

The primary concern of the document is with the practicalities involved with the renewal of the liturgy. Once again, this is not to say that the doctrinal aspect is neglected. To the contrary, the official eucharistic doctrine which was already firmly established by the time of the Council, is quite evidently the basis of the entire document. The official doctrine is also extensively stated in *The Roman Catechism* which was published in accordance with Vatican II and post-conciliar documents.[9] However, in an attempt to *clarify* the meaning and significance of the doctrine of the eucharist, the vast majority of the *Constitution on the Sacred Liturgy* is devoted to the renewal of the liturgy.

2. Active Participation

The purpose behind renewing the liturgy is evident at first glance: "In the restoration and promotion of the sacred liturgy this full and active participation by all people is the aim to be considered before all else . . ."[10] Active participation of all those present at the eucharistic celebration is the dominant theme which runs throughout the *Constitution*. It has in fact been referred to as the refrain of the *Constitution*, since it occurs a total of fifteen times in the document.[11]

This same theme is also repeated at great length in many of the post-conciliar documents. In his address to the United States bishops in 1978, for example, Pope Paul VI admonishes: "All the pastoral endeavors of our ministry are incomplete until the people that we are called to serve are led to full and active participation in the Eucharist."[12]

The conviction that participation in the liturgy is a right and duty of all people is made clear in the *Constitution*: "Such participation by the Christian people as "a chosen race, a royal priesthood, a holy nation, a purchased people" (1 Pet. 2:9; cf. 2:4-5), is their right and duty by reason of their baptism."[13] By virtue of baptism, all people share in the priesthood and are thereby called to worship God by actively participating in the liturgy.

Moreover, participation in the liturgy is essential if the liturgy is to fully effect the grace which is contained therein:

> In order that the sacred liturgy may produce its full effect, it is necessary that the faithful come to it with proper dispositions, that their thoughts match their words, and that they cooperate with divine grace lest they receive it in vain.[14]

While grace is always present to those who attend the liturgy as long as the sacramental action is validly performed, the benefits of that grace are received most fully through active and faith-filled participation. In this way, the eucharist becomes less an object and more a two way celebration of sanctification *and* worship.

3. People of God: The Christian Community

Vatican II's new vision of the church as the pilgrim people of God proved to be a major influence on the notion of active participation in the liturgy.[15] Before the Council, the term "Church" was often thought to be synonymous with clergy. With the development of the idea of people of God, however, the essential role of the laity is restored. The *Dogmatic Constitution on the Church*, issued on 21 November 1964, gives clear witness to the equality of laypeople in the Church:

> [Laypeople] are by baptism made one body with Christ and are established among the People of God. They are in their own way made sharers in the priestly, prophetic, and kingly functions of Christ . . . Therefore, the chosen People of God is one: "one Lord, one faith, one baptism" (Eph. 4:5). As members, they share a common dignity from their rebirth in Christ. They have the same filial grace and the same vocation to perfection. They possess in common one salvation, one hope, and one undivided charity.[16]

The notion of people of God marks the return to a communitarian theology of church. It emphasizes that the church is not made up of two separate entities—clergy and laity—but rather of one people. As a result, the layperson ". . . now enters the church building not as a second-class citizen, but as a living member of that primary category that God first called to the work of salvation, viz., the People of God . . ."[17]

Nowhere should this equality between laity and clergy be more evident than in the liturgy. By baptism in Christ, all are called to take part in His worship. This does not mean, of course, that the distinctive role of the hierarchical priesthood is to be eliminated. It does mean, however, that the liturgy should not be an isolated action of the priest at which the faithful remain passive, but an action in which all members of the Church play a distinctive role:

> Therefore liturgical services pertain to the whole body of the Church; they manifest it and have effects upon it; but they concern individual members of the Church in different ways, according to the diversity of holy orders, functions, and degrees of participation.[18]

Active participation by *all* members of the church is therefore a necessity.

In keeping with this new understanding of the church as the people of God, great emphasis is placed on the primacy of the Christian community. As a result, the *Constitution on the Sacred Liturgy* indicates that a communal celebration is to be preferred over a private ceremony:

> It is to be stressed that whenever rites, according to their specific nature, make provision for communal celebration involving the presence and active participation of the faithful, this way of celebrating them is to be preferred, as far as possible, to a celebration that is individual and quasi-private.[19]

With this emphasis on community, the individualistic piety which had perceived the liturgy to be a source of individual salvation is replaced by an understanding of the liturgy as an act of fellowship which incorporates the participants into a community with one another in and through Christ: "Now, however, the emphasis has shifted to viewing worship as a matter not simply of our own individual relations to God but of incorporation into Christ through and together with our neighbors."[20] The liturgy, therefore, must necessarily grow into a commemoration of Christ's Paschal Mystery that is celebrated by the entire community rather than simply the clergy. And, since it is the whole community that celebrates the eucharist, participation is an essential element.

4. Meaning of the Liturgy

The participants at Vatican II also found it necessary to explain at some length the meaning of the liturgy. Full participation in the liturgy, they claimed, cannot be achieved unless those who are called upon to participate have some understanding of what the liturgy is. Nor can we ". . . make active participation an end term or merely an external production."[21] The meaning of the liturgy must first be interiorized if active participation is to be authentic.

According to the Council, the liturgy derives its meaning from the celebration of the Paschal Mystery of Christ through which God revealed His love:

> From that time onward the Church has never failed to come together to celebrate the paschal mystery: reading "in all scriptures the things referring to himself" (Lk. 24:27), celebrating the Eucharist in which "the victory and triumph of his death are again made present," and at the same time giving thanks "to God for his unspeakable gift" (2 Cor. 9:15) in Christ Jesus, "to the praise of his glory" (Eph. 1:12), through the power of the Holy Spirit.[22]

In other words, the liturgy makes the Passion, the Resurrection and Ascension of Christ present to us today. It is the sacramental re-enactment of Christ's Paschal mystery which accomplishes in each celebration that which was once accomplished. Through the liturgy, the salvation won by Christ's death is continued by the Church which shares in His life. Thus, "the effects of the paschal mystery of Christ's passion, resurrection, and ascension and of His sending of the Holy Spirit are renewed whenever His people assemble for participation in liturgical celebration."[23]

5. Multiple Presences of Christ in the Liturgy

One of the most remarkable ways in which the theology of Vatican II impacted on the whole area of eucharistic theology was the expanded understanding of the real presence of Christ. While centuries upon centuries of conflicts and misunderstanding compelled Church theologians to pay primary significance to the real presence of Christ in the elements of bread and wine, theologians who had great influence at Vatican II began to view Christ's presence from a much broader perspective. Article 7 of the *Constitution on the Sacred Liturgy* provides ample evidence of this shift:

> Christ is always present in His Church, especially in her liturgical celebrations. He is present in the sacrifice of the Mass, not only in the person of His minister, "the same one now offering, through the ministry of priests, who formerly offered himself on the cross," but especi-

ally under the Eucharistic species. By His power He is
present in the sacraments, so that when a man baptizes
it is really Christ himself who baptizes. He is present
in His word, since it is he Himself who speaks when
the holy Scriptures are read in the Church. He is present finally when the Church prays and sings, for He
promised: "Where two or three are gathered together
for my sake, there am I in the midst of them" (Mt.
18:20)[24]

According to this understanding, Christ is present not only
under the eucharistic species, but throughout the entire liturgical celebration: in the person of the minister, the proclamation
of the word, the celebration of the other sacraments, the gathering of the community and its songs and prayers. The perception of the real presence of Christ has, therefore, been expanded
far beyond the traditional understanding.

This emphasis on the multiple presences of Christ in the
liturgy, according to Joseph Powers, marks a return to a more
Pauline theology of celebration. The eucharist is understood
not simply as the bread and wine, but rather as the entire
communal liturgical celebration. "In the theology of celebration, the presence of Jesus to and in his community is real and
effective in the whole action of the Eucharist . . . the presence
of Christ is seen as the enlivening power in the minister, congregation, Word, song and prayer."[25] With this understanding,
the real presence of Christ is recognized at the *heart* of the entire active eucharistic community. As a result, the real presence becomes less static and objectified.

This emphasis on the multiple presences of Christ in the
liturgy also leads to a new perspective on the conversion that
occurs in the eucharist. By acknowledging the fact that Christ
is present throughout the *entire* ritual, the understanding of
the eucharistic conversion cannot help but be altered. If the
presence of Christ is to be focused more broadly in the entire
communal celebration, that presence cannot be attributed only
to the conversion of bread and wine—transubstantiation. It
must also include that transformation which has happened
and is happening in the daily lives of those who participate in
the liturgy. In Powers' own words:

> . . . the "substance" which is to be changed is not only
> the substance of bread and wine. The "substance"

which is changed in the Eucharistic community is the entire life of the community which gathers for celebration of the Eucharist . . . "Transubstantiation" takes place as the substance of people's daily lives are changed by works of charity, piety and by the ministry which is given to each in their baptism.[26]

Instead of the bread and wine remaining the only focus of conversion, attention is also given to the transformation of the lives of the community members. The eucharist, then, should express and reflect this transformation.

In no way, however, does the eucharistic theology which resulted from Vatican II detract from the distinctiveness of the real presence of Christ in the bread and wine. To the contrary, the *Constitution* insists that Christ is present *especially* under the eucharistic species. However, in light of the fact that the eucharistic presence had been so highly emphasized in previous centuries, Vatican II itself does not dwell on it. In fact, by 1965, Paul VI found it necessary to strongly reaffirm the distinctiveness of Christ's presence in the species. In *Mysterium Fidei*, he adamantly declares that, although there are many authentic modes of presence, Christ is present above all in the eucharistic species. "This presence," he proclaims, "is called 'real' not to exclude the idea that the others are 'real' too, but rather to indicate presence *par excellence*, because it is substantial and through it Christ becomes present whole and entire, God and man."[27] Once again, the traditional belief in the real presence of Christ in the bread and wine is affirmed by the pronouncement that the eucharistic presence is unique because it alone contains Christ in the fullest sense.

The *Constitution* also clearly affirms that the real presence of Christ in the bread and wine is in fact the *cornerstone* of Christ's presence in the rest of the liturgy: "Christ's abiding presence in the whole Church has as its pre-eminent sacrament (effective cause and manifestation) the Eucharistic presence."[28] The real presence of Christ in the eucharistic species provides the basis for the presence of Christ in the rest of the liturgical celebration. While all modes of presence are real and authentic, the eucharistic presence is paramount.

The degree to which the reservation and adoration of the sacrament are encouraged in both conciliar and post-conciliar documents is yet another proof of the supremacy of the real presence in the bread and wine. Paul VI, for example, in an epistle to a eucharistic congress, adamantly declares that: "He remains in the hosts that are reserved after consecration as the bread of life that came down from heaven and under the veils of that sacrament he is worthy of divine worship in reverence and in the homage of adoration."[29] Statements such as these provide us with both a recognition of the permanency of Christ's presence in the sacrament and the uniqueness of that eucharistic presence.

Despite the appropriateness of reservation and adoration of the eucharist, however, the Church must never lose sight of the fact that Christ instituted the eucharist as spiritual nourishment to strengthen us and draw us into close communion with Him and His Church.[30] The emphasis, therefore, must never be on the permanent, static fact of the real presence, but on the communion for which it was instituted: "The real presence in the host is for the sake of the real presence in communion and the real presence in communion is for the sake of the real presence abiding in the Christian and in the body of Christians."[31]

6. The Liturgy as Sanctification and Worship

The *Constitution on the Sacred Liturgy* declares that the liturgy is a two-way movement between God and people that includes both the sanctification of people by God and the glorification of God through communal worship. Participants in the liturgy are made holy, first of all, because "they are given access to the stream of divine grace which flows from the paschal mystery of the passion, death and resurrection of Christ."[32] The liturgy also glorifies God insofar as it ". . . is above all things the worship of the divine Majesty."[33]

While the Council participants make it clear that the liturgy should be a two-way movement, for many centuries this simply was not a reality. The perception of the eucharist as worship was one which had been sorely neglected in much of the official Roman Catholic eucharistic theology. Of post-Tridentine theology, Liam Walsh explains: "it expounded admirably the sanctifying efficacy [of the sacraments], that downward movement by which grace comes from God to the soul, through the intrinsic power of a validly celebrated sacrament. But it tended to see the upward movement of worship only in the sacrificial aspect of the Mass."[34] The emphasis was on personal sanctification to the neglect of all else. Conciliar theology, on the other hand, stresses the idea that the liturgy is an encounter between God who reveals Himself in the eucharistic celebration and the participants who are called upon to respond in the liturgy through their prayers and songs of praise and thanksgiving. The ultimate meaning of the liturgy—God's glorification—is achieved by the sanctification of the people who are gathered to worship.

7. The Practicalities of Active Participation

In order for God to be glorified through worship, full and active participation by all members of the community is obviously a necessity. The *Constitution* explains in great detail how this full and active participation can be achieved.

Education

As the center and summit of the whole Christian life, the liturgy needs to be understood by all. Hence, the basis set out by the *Constitution on the Sacred Liturgy* is the liturgical instruction and education of all who are present at the liturgy. Participation is impossible if the liturgy is unintelligible to those who are in attendance. While the primary aim of liturgical instruction is undoubtedly the laypeople, the emphasis of the document is on the education of the clergy. In Article 14, for example, it is declared:

> Yet it would be futile to entertain any hopes of realizing this goal unless the pastors themselves, to begin with, become thoroughly penetrated with the spirit and power of the liturgy, and become masters of it. It is vitally necessary, therefore, that attention be directed above all, to the liturgical instruction of the clergy.

All clergy are to be well instructed in the study of the liturgy in order that they may in turn give instruction to the laypeople.

The hoped-for result of this is, of course, the knowing, active participation of all who attend the liturgy.

Revision of the rite

The most important advocation of the Council is the revision of the rite of the liturgy, since it is by this revision that active participation can most effectively be accomplished:

> The rite of the Mass is to be revised in such a way that the intrinsic nature and purpose of its several parts, as also the connection between them, can be more clearly manifested, and that devout and active participation by the faithful can be more easily accomplished. For this purpose the rites are to be simplified, while due care is taken to preserve their substance.[35]

According to the *Constitution*, elements which are no longer functional or meaningful to those present are to be changed or excluded. "In this restoration," Article 21 admonishes, "both texts and rites should be drawn up so that they express more clearly the holy things which they signify. Christian people, as far as possible, should be able to understand them with ease and to take part in them fully, actively, and as befits a community." Greater simplicity and authenticity are thereby the key to revision.

With regards to the actual implementation of this revision, however, caution is advised. In fact, certain rules are laid down for the changes:

> That sound tradition may be retained, and yet the way be open for legitimate progress, a careful investigation is always to be made into each part of the liturgy which is to be revised. This investigation should be theological, historical, and pastoral . . . there must be no innovations unless the good of the Church genuinely and certainly require them.[36]

Hence, both tradition and progress are to be priorities.

Furthermore, the rites themselves are to be explained to all present in order that the people gain an understanding of the meaning behind the ritual. They cannot remain outer ceremonies, but must become inner experiences for each person that forms the community. "If we cannot discover the essential core, the hidden reality that takes place under the veil of the external liturgical event, the liturgy will never become for us a meeting, a prayer."[37] Thus, the liturgy is not meant to be an empty ritual, but a meaningful and authentic experience of worship.

Emphasis on the Word

Another part of the revision of the eucharistic liturgy is a new emphasis on the vital importance of God's word in the liturgy: "Sacred Scripture is of paramount importance in the celebration of the liturgy . . . Thus if restoration, progress, and adaptation of the sacred liturgy are to be achieved, it is necessary to promote that warm and living love for Scripture."[38] After the minor role given to Scripture for so many years, the conciliar statement gives it a place of equal importance with the eucharist. Thus, Christ *is* present not only under the eucharistic species, but in His word as well. The homily, in addition, is to be included as an extension or continuation of God's word. Like Scripture, its task is not only to proclaim the mystery of Christ, but also to instruct the participants in the "mysteries of the faith and the guiding principles of the Christian life."[39]

Reintroduction of the prayer of the faithful

According to the *Constitution*, the prayer of the faithful is also to be re-introduced into the liturgy. By this means, all people can participate in the worship of God by bringing to Him their own concerns and needs. Indeed,

> The re-introduction of the common prayer met at once with approval in the Council. This is not surprising because it is an element in which the participation of the faithful finds expression in a remarkable way, both as regards its content, in that it takes up the concerns felt by all, and also as regards its form as a prayer with responses.[40]

Moreover, all those present are encouraged to take an active role, not only in the prayer of the faithful, but in other prayers and responses as well: "by way of promoting active participation, the people should be encouraged to take part by means of acclamations, responses, psalmody, antiphons and songs."[41]

Use of the Vernacular

One of the most influential and far-reaching changes officially endorsed by the Council is the use of the vernacular. The use of the mother tongue is seen as a primary means by which all might take an active role in the liturgy:

> But since the use of the mother tongue, whether in the Mass, the administration of the sacraments, or other parts of the liturgy, may frequently be of great advantage to the people, the limits of its employment may be extended. This extension will apply in the first place to the readings and directives, and to some of the prayers and chants.[42]

While extended, the use of the vernacular is nonetheless to be limited to those parts of the liturgy which pertain in particular to the laypeople. The notable exception here, of course, is the Canon of the Mass: article 54 explicitly states that the Ordinary of the Mass must remain in Latin. An interesting point to keep in mind, however, is that the wording of article 54 was deliberately left vague in deference to those who were opposed to any use of the vernacular. In response to the conflict between those who wanted to completely exclude any use of the mother tongue and those who advocated a complete change to it, the Council left it to the discretion of the local bishops to determine the extent to which the vernacular could be used.[43]

As can be imagined, the use of the vernacular is a major impetus for the full participation of those present at the liturgy. There is little doubt that when the Mass was said in Latin—a language which proved to be almost incomprehensible for the majority of the laypeople—most people attended the liturgy as passive spectators rather than active participants. Moreover, the liturgy itself became the occasion to develop an isolated and individualistic spirituality. Those present could not understand the language and often tended to become engrossed in their own private devotions. Participation in the liturgy was at a minimum.

The Council's endorsement of the vernacular presents the ideal opportunity for all people to understand and take part in what is happening at the liturgical celebration. Furthermore, the fact that all people can now take part in the liturgy helps to emphasize the fact that the liturgy is a *communal* act of worship. Private devotions during Mass are to be replaced by communal prayers and responses. Most significantly, the use of the mother tongue also serves to cut down the barrier between the priest and the people. Rather than the liturgy being a one-man action in which the priest addresses those present in a foreign tongue, the vernacular would serve to illustrate the character of dialogue in which the priest leads and the people respond.[44]

Rite of Communion

The Council also sought to achieve the full participation of those present at the liturgy by revising the rite of communion of the eucharist. Two aspects are most notable. First, Article 55 declares that: "hearty endorsement is given to that closer form of participation in the Mass whereby the faithful, after the priest's communion, receive the Lord's body under the elements consecrated at that very sacrifice." The bread and wine consecrated at the celebration are to be received sacramentally by those who are present at that liturgy. The reception of the real presence of Christ in the elements is given priority over the reservation and adoration of the consecrated host. Moreover, the fact that the liturgy is a meal in which all are called to play an active role is thereby emphasized. As a result, active participation in the liturgy is intensified. Most importantly, this once again aids in breaking down the barrier between priest and people that was erected when the priest communed at the altar and then used the hosts from the tabernacle for the rest of the people. "If the people now communicate with hosts taken from the tabernacle," Adrian Hastings explains, "the priest has to walk away from the altar after his own communion to fetch them and the impression of a divorce between the sacrifice and communion, and between the priest's communion and the people's communion, is made still worse."[45] To partake together of the same hosts is a powerful indication that the communion of the layperson is as full and valid as that of the priest.

Revision of the rite of communion also includes the admonition that, in certain circumstances, all those present may communicate under both species. Without rejecting Trent's declaration that Christ is wholly present under either species,

Vatican II nonetheless declares: "Communion under both kinds may be granted when the bishops think fit, not only to clerics and religious, but also to the laity, in cases to be determined by the Apostolic See."[46] Communion of both bread and wine helps to more fully express the sense of full participation in the eucharistic banquet: reception of both species makes the sign value of the sacrament more manifest since Christ did command His apostles to eat *and* drink. "Communion under both kinds is not fuller at the level of the thing signified, but it is fuller and more complete at the level of the sign itself; and it is the level of the sign, the sacrament itself, that the Church has primarily to concern herself with."[47] And, once again, an artificial barrier between priest and laypeople will be broken down. When the chalice is not given to the people, but reserved only for the cleric, the impression is created that the layperson's communion is not as full or important as that of the clerics. Communion under both species for the laity will, therefore, "make clear that the participation of the laity in Holy Communion is as complete as that of the clerics."[48]

Conclusion

The twentieth century liturgical movement has resulted in a major shift in emphasis on the part of the official Roman Catholic Church. From being concerned almost solely with the refining, exposition and declaration of eucharistic doctrine as was the case in previous centuries, the church of the twentieth century has become more and more aware of the need to officially promote the active participation of all people present at the liturgy. This emphasis can be recognized especially in the conciliar documents of Vatican II, which state as their aim the reform of the liturgy in order to achieve active participation. As a result, the laypeople are being recognized as a necessary and vital component. Rather than the attention being focused on the eucharist as a solitary action of the priest, all laypeople are called upon to assume a prominent and active role in the entire liturgical celebration. Moreover, in previous centuries the eucharist was understood primarily in terms of causality. That which was deemed to be of supreme importance was the objective conferral of grace achieved by the fact of the real presence and the sacrifice of Christ in the Mass. With the advent of Vatican II, however, the causality of the eucharist, although not neglected, does not receive the overemphasis that it had in former centuries. Instead, more attention is placed on the value of the eucharist as an instructive sign which emphasizes that the eucharist is a sacrificial banquet in and of which all those present are to participate and partake.

Many of the changes which were recommended at Vatican II have far exceed expectations. The use of the vernacular, far from being limited, is almost universal. Communion under both species, likewise, is increasingly becoming the norm in many parishes.

Despite official sanctioning, however, it is taking many decades of cautious refining before the final results are achieved. In the meantime, it is becoming more and more apparent that modern Roman Catholics are beginning to take a stance that makes evident their need to discover and understand the *meaning* that lies behind the doctrine of the eucharist so that they can in fact partake of the eucharist as active participants. These people are beginning to recognize that that which frustrates them and robs the eucharist of joy for them is the lack of meaning and relevance. To this end, they are striving to arrive at a new understanding of the eucharist which, without going beyond the bounds of orthodoxy, will go beyond a purely objective and factual understanding of the eucharist in terms of the real presence and the sacrifice of the Mass and thereby give the eucharist a new meaning that is much more relevant to the modern layperson. This quest, I would suggest, is an attempt to liberate the eucharist from its traditional trappings, and, in so doing, to speed up the process begun at Vatican II of returning the eucharist to the ordinary Roman Catholic. It is, therefore, an attempt to allow the laypeople to understand the meaning of that which they celebrate in the eucharistic liturgy in order that they might participate in it joyfully and willingly, rather than out of a sense of obligation.

Discussion Questions

1. What is the major focus of the *Constitution on the Sacred Liturgy*? Why is it primary?

2. Why is a theological and doctrinal basis a necessity for eucharistic reform?

3. What was the understanding of the church which arose from the Council? How does this affect the celebration of the eucharist?

4. How has the perception of the real presence of Christ been expanded in the *Constitution on the Sacred Liturgy*? Why is this expansion significant?

5. What is meant by the statement: "The liturgy is a two way movement between God and people"? How does this differ from the pre-Vatican II understanding of the liturgy?

6. Name the changes in the celebration of the eucharist which were mandated at Vatican II. Which are most significant to you? Why?

7. How have some of the changes advocated at Vatican II been implemented? Been developed even further? What things do you now take for granted which were a novelty in the 1960's?

8. List some major differences between the pre-Vatican II and the post-Vatican II understandings of Church? Of laity? Of eucharist?

9. If you were asked to reform the eucharistic liturgy even further, what changes would you make? Explain.

Chapter Three

The Eucharist—A Personal Encounter with Christ

DURING THE YEARS OF THE SECOND VATICAN COUNCIL, as well as in those immediately following, it became clear that a number of theologians were taking seriously the Council's call to reform. As a result, they grappled with ways to make the eucharist more meaningful for all those who joined together for the eucharistic celebration. This is not to say, of course, that such a movement arose only at that time. Rather, the years of 1964 and 1965 marked the era when specifically Catholic attempts at reinterpretation became widely known to the Church as a whole.[1] From Western Europe in particular, there arose a dominant school of Roman Catholic theologians who argued the need to reinterpret the Tridentine dogma of transubstantiation. The grounds? The medieval terms by which the dogma was expressed were of little or no relevance to the twentieth century person and often tended to be a hindrance to a proper understanding of the meaning of the eucharist. While striving to maintain the meaning contained in the dogma, these theologians endeavoured to shift the emphasis away from the objective categories in which the real presence of Christ in the eucharist was previously expressed to the more personal and subjective categories of the encounter with the living Christ which the real presence entails. It was an attempt to make the eucharist more meaningful for those who partake of it.

> All wish to safeguard the authentic doctrine. They wish, however, to safeguard it in such a way that the people of God, especially the clergy, formed more and more in a non-scholastic mentality, might live it in a more authentic fashion and, so to speak, in a more existential manner.[2]

Historical Background

The reinterpretation of the eucharist which became prevalent in 1964 and 1965 was preceded by a number of years during which different aspects influencing the new theology were being developed. In fact, subtle traces of this attempt at reinterpretation can be found as early as the 1930's.[3] It was not, however, until the ten years immediately following the publication of *Humani Generis* by Pius XII in 1950 that theologians began to develop a number of new ideas which ultimately had a great impact on the change of approach to eucharistic theology that became prevalent especially in 1964 and 1965.[4]

1. The Influence of Modern Physics

From 1949 to 1956, a series of articles exchanged by F. Selvaggi and C. Columbo forced theologians to consider whether or not theology should enter into dialogue with science. This question in turn prepared the ground for theologians to deal more specifically with the issue of how and if atomic physics was related to the eucharistic conversion as described by Trent.[5]

The theological debate commenced in 1949 when Selvaggi published an article in which he articulated the need for theologians to look at transubstantiation in light of these findings of modern physics. He challenged them to determine whether the terms used by Trent should be understood in a physical sense or at a metaphysical level. His own view was that transubstantiation *must* be understood in terms of physical conceptions of reality and be readily explainable to a scientist. The consequence of this assertion, however, was startling. By agreeing with the scientist that bread is not one simple substance but rather is made up of thousands of molecular structures, Selvaggi claimed that the theologian must be prepared to explain how the conversion of the bread into Christ's body takes place—as a whole or as components of the whole. Selvaggi's response, ludicrous as it may seem, was clear: for the thousands of particles which make up the substance of bread, there must be a corresponding number of transubstantiations.[6] Thus, for Selvaggi, the change which takes place in the eucharist was in fact on the physical level; the physical reality of the bread, he would claim, was part of transubstantiation.[7] With little change, this is the position that he upheld throughout the next decade of challenge and controversy.

Six years after the 1949 article, Selvaggi's view was challenged in a series of articles written by Msgr. Carlo Colombo. Like many others, Colombo insisted that modern physics had no place within theology. In dealing with transubstantiation, theologians are dealing with a metaphysical reality far beyond the parameters of physics: "The reality of the substance of the bread, as well as of the body of Christ, is a metaphysical reality and as such is completely beyond the scope of the physical scientist, who is concerned with the accidental character, or species, of things."[8] The term substance, as it is used in eucharistic theology, is a theological term which tradition (Aquinas, for example) has placed on a metaphysical level. "Hence, the change takes place between realities that are beyond scientific investigation, that is, metaphysical realities."[9] While physics may be capable of addressing the issue of bread and wine on a physical level, it cannot speak to a change of substance, since tradition has dictated that substance is on a completely different level of reality.

These, then, are the two main positions in the debate. "Once the initial positions were adopted, there was little change on either side outside of some refinement."[10] The controversy was, as most scholars contend, long, complex, convoluted and often exaggerated.[11] Its importance, however, lies in the fact that theologians were forced to acknowledge, at least to a certain extent, the relation between physics and eucharistic theology, an issue which proved to be of significance in later years.

> Of itself, this Selvaggi-Colombo debate, that was joined of course, by theologians of that day, led nowhere. Nonetheless, the issue that it raised influenced in no small degree a number of other theologians who eventually became associated with the term "transsignification."[12]

2. Rediscovery of the Sacramental Symbolic Activity

The years before the Second Vatican Council also marked the rediscovery of the sacramental symbolic activity. In post World War II theology, emphasis was again being given to the fact that the sacraments are symbolic acts. The Council of Trent, in reaction to the Reformers, emphasized the causality of the sacraments. As a result, causality and sign value were put into opposition and the sign value of the sacraments fell into obscurity.[13] It was not until the years after the Second World War that there began to emerge a re-appreciation of the eucharistic sign.

To a great extent, modern phenomenology added to the rediscovery of the sign value of the sacraments. Phenomenology seeks to discover and analyze the essential meaning of something as it appears within human experience rather than from metaphysical categories:

> More important than the question of what a thing is in itself or substantially is the question of what it means within its relationship to human existence and the way in which we from our human standpoint can unlock this meaning."[14]

Considered from this point of view, the reality of the sign can then be situated in an anthropology of the symbolic act. Perhaps an analogy is useful at this point: a sign is like a person whose inner spirituality is made visible in the way that person directs himself or herself outwards towards other persons and the world. The human person, then, is experienced directly in those actions. Understood in terms of the sacraments, ". . . the reality itself can be experienced directly in human symbolic action."[15] As a result, the sacraments can then be taken out of the material level of things and taken up into the personal level.

The work done by J. de Baciocchi was one of the earliest attempts to situate the eucharist in the sphere of symbolic activity without giving it a purely symbolic interpretation. De Baciocchi's starting point was the assertion that the real presence must never be understood as an isolated reality. Rather, Christ's presence in the eucharist *must* be seen within the context of Christ's gift of himself to the Church. Basing his argument on the assumption that Christ's action of giving bread and wine both signifies and actualizes Christ's gift of himself to the Church, De Baciocchi argued that the bread and wine on the altar become the *efficacious signs* by which Christ's gift of himself to the Church is both explained and accomplished.[16]

After affirming the fact of the real presence, De Baciocchi explored the manner in which the bread and wine become effective signs of Christ's gift to the Church. The empirical reality of the bread and wine, he asserted, do not change: volume, weight, taste, physical and chemical properties remain unaltered, on the level at which our senses grasp reality. By the power of Christ's word, however, the social and religious reality of the bread and wine are changed into the real sign of Christ's body and blood.[17] The bread becomes, in reality, Christ's body because that is the value which Christ has given to it by virtue of the words of consecration. That which is of importance, then, is the value which Christ gives to something.

This is not to say, however, that an objective fundamental change has not taken place in the reality of those elements. Rather, De Bachiocchi insisted that insofar as the bread and wine become the real sign of Christ's presence, this change does indeed merit the name "transubstantiation."[18] Despite the awkwardness of the term "substance" in today's world, transubstantiation does have a positive value: it affirms that the bread and wine, which remain bread and wine on the empirical level, truly and objectively become the body and blood of Christ. While adding nothing new to Christ's words at the Last Supper, transubstantiation, as De Baciocchi understood it, ". . . formulates the only possible way of establishing complete accord between the eucharistic gift and the testimony of the senses on the one hand, and the principle of identity on the other."[19]

3. Re-Interpretation of the Tridentine Concept of Substance

Closely related to the rediscovery of the sign value of the eucharist was the attempt by several theologians to determine exactly what Trent mean by the term "substance." E. Gutwenger, on the one hand, maintained that Trent did in fact make Aristotelian concepts a necessary component of Catholic faith in the real presence.[20] On the other hand, G. Ghysens insisted that Trent consciously disassociated itself from the Aristotelian concept of substance by using the term in the very general sense of "fundamental reality."[21] Edward Schillebeeckx agrees with neither: "the dogma was thought out and expressed in "Aristotelian" categories, but the strictly Aristotelian content of these categories was not included in what the dogma intended to say."[22] While such a debate will likely never be settled to everyone's satisfaction, its significance lies in the fact that more and more theologians were openly expressing their dissatisfaction with the concept of substance. This, in turn, had a profound impact on the acceptance of the term "transubstantiation" by which Roman Catholic belief in the real presence was expressed.

4. Emphasis on the Manifold Presence of Christ

The 1950's and 1960's also marked a return to the biblical and liturgical emphases on the manifold presence of Christ within the whole scope of Christian life, rather than the Tridentine concentration on the real presence of Christ in the species. This renewed recognition that Christ's real presence cannot be limited to the eucharistic presence was given official status first by the Council participants at Vatican II in the *Constitution on the Sacred Liturgy* and then by Paul VI in *Mysterium Fidei*.

According to these official documents, Christ is really present in *all* the sacraments. Moreover, Christ is really, personally present in anyone (not only the priest) who is in a state of grace. In fact, according to Edward Kilmartin, the documents even go so far as to maintain that ". . . the presence of Christ in the believer, as sharing source of faith in his abiding presence, is basic to all other modes of personal presence of Christ in the Church."[23] In the context of the eucharistic liturgy, Christ is really present in the assembly and prayers of the faithful and in the service of the word. Finally, and most specifically, he is really present in the elements of bread and wine at the eucharist.

The recognition of the multiple presences of Christ was in no way meant to disparage the eucharistic presence. Rather, ". . . faith in the eucharistic presence of Christ is not belittled but heightened by our faith awareness of Christ's real presence in the assembly, his word and in the person of his minister."[24] Moreover, as Schillebeeckx insisted, this was a return to an awareness of the purpose for which Christ does become present in the elements: a more intimate presence in the heart of the Christian and the Christian community. Hence, "the eucharistic presence is thus no longer isolated. We no longer say, 'Christ is there,' without asking for whom he is present."[25]

5. Ecumenical Movement

The ecumenical movement of post World War II Europe was also a major impetus to the rethinking of Roman Catholic eucharistic doctrine. Theologians on both sides—Roman Catholic and Protestant—were starting to exchange a certain number of ideas. Many Roman Catholic theologians began to recognize that a re-thinking of certain presuppositions and terms was necessary if open contact with other denominations was to be maintained. Moreover, the recognition of the validity of non-Catholic communities as grace-filled Churches led to a logical conclusion: the recognition of the authenticity of their theology. "The Protestant experience of the eucharist," Schillebeeckx (among others) concludes, "must therefore be taken into account by Catholic theologians."[26] In light of this discovery, the eucharistic theology of F.J. Leenhardt in particular proved to be a great influence on Roman Catholic theologians.

The point of departure for Leenhardt's inquiry into transubstantiation was the conviction that the essential reality of a thing is dependent on what God wills to make of it in order to realize His purpose of creative love for humanity:

> In other words, the true reality of things is to be found in what God wishes them to be for His creatures . . . What things are in the final analysis is what God gives through them to man . . . the essence of a reality lies in the divine intention which is realized through it.[27]

Drawing upon this concept of reality, Leenhardt went beyond the purely metaphysical definition of substance that was the framework of the dogma of transubstantiation. "Substance is the final reality of things as faith recognizes it in God's creation and in His ordinance to His creatures."[28] For Leenhardt, substance did not mean the matter behind the accidents, but the final reality that God wills an object to be. Transubstantiation, then, could be accepted, as long as it was not understood in Aristotelian terms.[29]

The implication of this concept of reality for the doctrine of the eucharist was that the words of Christ give the bread a new meaning and therefore transform its substance into his body.[30] By declaring "This is my Body," Christ expresses the final reality of the bread.

> He pronounces over it a word which expresses what the final destiny of this bread shall henceforth be. He brings it about that this bread has no longer its final reason for existence in the nourishment of the body. . . . What is essential in this bread which Christ gives, declaring that it is His body, is not what the baker has made of it, but what Jesus Christ has made of it when He gives it and declares that it is His body.[31]

While remaining unchanged on the material level, the substance of the bread has, by virtue of God's will, become the instrument of Christ's presence. Transubstantiation, albeit understood on a different level, had occurred.

Theology of the Sacraments

During this time as well, the whole area of sacramental theology began to undergo a complete shift in emphasis. Moving beyond the traditional understanding of sacraments as instruments of divine grace conferred by God through an act of the church, theologians began to insist that the sacraments be understood as personal saving encounters between humans and God. Since it is in light of such an understanding of the sacraments that one must examine the development of eucharistic theology that emerged in the 1960's, attention will now be focused on the work of two of the leading proponents of the renewal of sacramental theology: Edward Schillebeeckx and Karl Rahner.

1. Theology of Grace

The starting point for this new understanding of the sacraments is the presupposition that grace is present in all aspects of human life; that is, personal saving encounters between God and humanity take place everywhere in everyday life.[32] God does not, according to this new conception of grace, "insert" grace into an otherwise ungraced world by means of certain divine actions. "God is . . . not an outsider to human life, a God up there or out there, who from time to time perforates the fabric of human history by means of spectacularly interventionist incursions."[33] Rather, God is present in every aspect of life and in the history of the whole world. The world is, therefore, already permeated with grace.

The impact of such a presupposition on the theology of the sacraments is tremendous. The belief that the world was evil or profane and that the sacraments were a primary means by which grace could be infused into such a world made frequent reception of the sacraments a necessity. Karl Rahner puts it in these words: "In order to get in touch with God, every now and then [one] steps out of this profane world into a "fane," a holy place . . . The sacrament alone puts [one] in touch with the Lord and makes [one's] life meaningful and "religious."[34] When faced with the belief that the world itself is graced by God's presence, then, the idea that the sacraments are discharges of grace into a profane world is no longer valid.

The sacraments are nevertheless useful and necessary to the Christian life insofar as they are a ". . . manifestation in one's own life of the grace that guides the history of the whole world."[35] Encountering God in the sacraments is an illumination of the encounter with God which can and does occur everywhere in the world in everyday life. The notion of what a sacrament is has thus been expanded far beyond previous definitions.

2. Christ: The Sacrament of God

At the basis of this expanded notion of sacrament lies the fundamental belief that Jesus himself is the primordial or basic sacrament. According to both Schillebeeckx and Rahner, the deepest manifestation of that grace which is part of everyday life can be found in the life and actions of Jesus of Nazareth. In his life and relationships with others, Jesus makes visible the grace of God. An encounter with the human Jesus is a sacrament insofar as it is a visible and historical sign of God's love and forgiveness for all people. And, since every bestowal of grace occurs as a result of an encounter with this human Jesus, he is the primordial sacrament, the fundamental sign of God's love. Schillebeeckx explains as follows:

> The man Jesus, as the personal visible realization of the divine grace of redemption, is the sacrament, the primordial sacrament, because this man, the Son of God himself, is intended by the Father to be in his humanity the only way to the actuality of redemption.[36]

Further expansion of the perception of sacraments exists in the discovery that there are two dimensions to every encounter with God: an invitation on God's part and a human response. Jesus, as the primordial sacrament of the encounter with God, fulfills both elements: he is, at one and the same time, a visible embodiment of God's self disclosure and the human response of love to that revelation:

> Jesus the Christ is the primordial sacrament because in him we find the fullest expression of what a sacrament is; the visible, audible, tangible expression of God's saving love for us and the human response to this love.[37]

Thus, Jesus himself is the basic or fundamental sacrament insofar as his very humanity gives both a tangible and personal form to God's loving acceptance of humankind and a manifestation of human response to that love.

3. The Church: The Sacrament of Christ

Following the assertion that Jesus is the primordial sacrament, both Schillebeeckx and Rahner claim that the Church is also a sacrament insofar as it is a sign of the on-going presence of the risen Christ. As a result of his death and resurrection, Jesus is no longer on earth in visible, historical form. Since an encounter with God can happen only by virtue of an encounter with the human Jesus, his glorified state would appear to pose a problem. This is not the case, however, since the Church is the visible prolongation of the saving reality of Jesus. Insofar as it signifies God's offer of himself through Christ to humanity, the Church is also a sacrament. Rahner explains the concept as follows: "As the ongoing presence of

Jesus Christ in time and space, as the fruit of salvation which can no longer perish, and as the means of salvation by which God offers his salvation to an individual in a tangible way and in the historical and social dimension, the church is the basic sacrament."[38] The Church, therefore, makes visible the risen Christ, who would otherwise be invisible and thus makes tangible the salvation offered by God in Christ. As a sign which continues to make God's saving love visible to humanity, the Church is a primordial sacrament.

The Church, too, fulfils both dimensions of an encounter with God: the invitation and the response. "Thus the Church in its own proper activity is a historical manifestation of God's own love for [people] in Christ (a bestowal of grace) and, at the same time, of its own love and adoration of God in the same Lord (worship)."[39] When its members are united in love to one another and to God, the Church itself becomes a sign of God's love for humanity. In its worship and its action, the Church also becomes the human response to this love.[40]

4. Toward a Definition of the Sacraments

It is on the basis of these two fundamental sacraments— Christ and the Church—that the seven ritual sacraments derive their sacramentality. "Christ is the sacrament of our encounter with God, and we achieve our sacramental encounter with Christ in the Church through the seven sacraments."[41] Christ and the Church are, then, wellsprings from which all the sacraments draw their power and the source to which the sacraments can be traced.

When the Church, as the historical manifestation of God's love in Christ, makes that love present at specific moments in human life, the result is the seven ritual sacraments. These seven sacraments are special gifts from God which make humanity aware of the experience of God's grace which is already a reality. "The sacraments proclaim and enable us to appropriate the love of God already present and offered to us."[42]

Part of this expanded understanding of sacrament includes the assertion that the sacraments are not primarily physical things, but rather, ". . . first and foremost symbolic acts or activity as signs."[43] Humans need visible, tangible signs of God's love and the seven sacraments provide these at different times in life. The encounter with God is thus expressed and made tangible in visible actions and physical things which point beyond themselves to the saving reality of Christ. As acts or signs of the Church, they are also acts and signs of Christ.

The seven sacraments do not merely consist of God's action, but also demand an indication of human response of faith and devotion. In fact, Richard Gula even goes so far as to claim:

> Sacraments are our need, not God's. The whole point of celebrating sacramentally is to provide human situations in which we can respond in a tangible and visible way to our experiences of God in Christ and the spirit and to our belonging to one another in community as the Body of Christ.[44]

For a sacrament to develop into a real personal encounter with Christ, human response is a necessity.

The Reinterpretation of the Eucharist

With this background in mind, we now turn our attention to the eucharistic theology which emerged during the 1960's.[45] For Edward Schillebeeckx, the most fundamental requirement is to make the dogma of transubstantiation relevant to the twentieth century person while still retaining its basic meaning. Because Catholic faith is a living faith that exists within the progress of history, it is necessary to go beyond a mere repetition of a dogma of faith which was developed in the past. In order to seize the full implications of transubstantiation, Schillebeeckx maintains, it is necessary

> . . . to reinterpret the world of ideas with which the dogma of transubstantiation has come down to us, precisely in order to be able to preserve in a pure form the

basic meaning of the dogma and to make it capable of being freshly experienced by modern man.[46]

In order to reinterpret the dogma of transubstantiation, it is first necessary to distinguish between that which was affirmed about the eucharistic presence at the Council of Trent and the way in which that affirmation was expressed. According to Schillebeeckx, that which emerged from Trent was an affirmation of a specific and distinctive presence of Christ which was brought about on the basis of a change of substance of bread and wine into Christ's body and blood, a change which was aptly named transubstantiation. This was, however, never meant to be two separate dogmas—one of the real presence and one of the substantial change—but simply one forceful statement of the real presence. Hence, he insists that ". . . the only aim of the Council of Trent was to proclaim the unique and distinctive character of the eucharistic presence as an inviolable datum of faith."[47]

The dogma of transubstantiation was used to express the central dogma of the real presence. With the passage of time, the two became so intertwined that a rejection of the substantial conversion was equated with a denial of the real presence. Schillebeeckx, however, argues that the idea of a real change (which is what Trent wished to affirm) is in fact separable from the term transubstantiation. Thus, the affirmation of the reality of the change that occurs in the eucharist can and must be distinguished from the Aristotelian concepts used to explain it without fear of affecting the doctrine of the real presence itself. Karl Rahner agrees: he insists that a distinction must be maintained between ". . . what on the one hand is precisely and clearly implied in the dogma of transubstantiation . . . and therefore belongs to the dogma, and as to what on the other hand only belongs to the theological explanation of the doctrine in terms of a given philosophical concept."[48] The truth expressed by the term transubstantiation can be meaningfully expressed in other terms as long as the truth of the reality of the change is maintained. It is possible, therefore, to preserve the truth of the Church's belief in a real change in the elements of the eucharist while reinterpreting it in terms which are relevant to the twentieth century person.

1. A New Point of Departure: Interpersonal Relationships

Rather than starting from the framework of natural philosophy, the new point of departure for eucharistic theology for Schillebeeckx and his contemporaries is that of anthropology or human meaning. "The way in which human beings at particular points in time and space perceive the world is of the utmost importance" for the new eucharistic theology.[49] In an attempt to make eucharistic theology more relevant to the modern Catholic, human perspective becomes the framework from which to work.

Laying the Foundations: Piet Schoonenberg and Charles Davis

Two theologians who were most instrumental in laying the foundations for the new framework, and to whom Schillebeeckx admits his indebtedness, are Piet Schoonenberg and Charles Davis. The proper context in which the eucharist should be discussed, they insist, is that of the dynamics of interpersonal relationships.

Schoonenberg's major contribution in this area is his analysis of the concept of presence. He begins by asserting that Christ is already personally present to humanity through the reality of grace in life. This personal presence is the highest form of presence: while spatial presence is simply a being in a place in a local way, personal presence is the presence of a person to a person, a relationship characterized by free self-determined communication and spiritual openness.[50] Furthermore, while there are different degrees of personal presence, only that presence which is both offered and accepted is brought to completion; only then does the relationship become interpersonal. Reciprocity is, therefore, an essential factor.

For humans, personal presence needs spatial presence to a certain degree. Without being totally dependent on it, personal presence does need spatial presence in order to come into existence; only if people meet first in a spatial way can they enter into a relationship.[51] In the case of Jesus' relationship to humanity, however, spatial presence is not a concern:

> In the case of Jesus also, we are not concerned with the spatial presence. This existed during his earthly life, but even then it was never important without his personal presence . . . Now that the Lord has been glorified, the spatial presence has been entirely done away with and the Lord is present everywhere where hearts believe in him.[52]

Christ is present to humanity by grace. Again, however, while Christ's offer is always open, it is only when this presence is accepted that an interpersonal relationship develops.

Charles Davis further augments this idea of relationship by affirming that this personal presence, this union with Christ through grace which is already an actuality, is deepened in the eucharist. The eucharist, therefore, both presupposes and expresses an already existing interpersonal relationship with Christ by grace: ". . . in the Eucharistic celebration Christ is really present to us in the full interpersonal sense, because this celebration is the embodiment and expression of his presence to us by grace."[53] The purpose of the eucharist, then, and that which gives it meaning, is the establishment of a deeper and more intimate relationship with Christ. In the celebration of the eucharist, Christ offers the gift of his body and blood and humanity accepts that offer. The emphasis is not on the presence of Christ in the eucharist but on the purpose of that presence: further intimacy with Christ. Thus, the eucharist ". . . is a personal encounter with Christ in which he once again offers us union with himself, and invites us closer, and in which we accept and draw nearer to him."[54]

In light of this understanding of the eucharist as a personal encounter with Christ, the real presence of Christ in the eucharist is perceived as only the first stage in the process of developing an interpersonal relationship: "It is a preliminary stage in the achievement of that mutual personal presence by which Christ is present to us and we to him."[55] Only when a person accepts that presence can an interpersonal relationship be achieved. The real presence of Christ in the eucharist can never, therefore, be made an objective end unto itself, since it ". . . is but a moment in the process of Christ's self-giving."[56] Human acceptance must always accompany Christ's offer of personal communion for an interpersonal relationship to develop.

Another dimension which results from working out of the framework of human meaning is the notion that reality is changed when humanity establishes new meaning for it. Once again, Charles Davis makes major contributions to this fundamental tenet. Bread, he insists, has no meaning, no existence, apart from its relationship to humanity. Bread itself is only a mixture of components, but "their unity and intelligibility come from the finality imposed on them by man, and not from any substantial change in the order of physical reality."[57] This does not mean to imply, of course, that reality is of human making. To the contrary, although an object is knowable according to its relation to humanity, the relation itself is given by God. E.L. Mascall summarizes Davis' thought: ". . . although the object is called bread . . . in view of its relation to man . . . the relation that is signified [is not] given to it by man; it is given by God. Relations to man, yes; relations established by man, no. The relation is established by God."[58]

2. What is Reality? Schillebeeckx' Basic Principles

These two tenets—that reality is not of human making, but of God's, and that this reality is given its meaning in relation to humanity—are the two basic principles from which Schillebeeckx operates. With Davis, Schillebeeckx maintains that humanity gives meaning to reality. This is not to say, of course, that reality is of human making, since one must always keep in mind that ". . . meanings given by man are governed by a reality which is . . . in the first place God's, and only then man's."[59] Indeed, given the example of creation, one can see that God gives the ultimate meaning of the world and that the initiative is God's. Furthermore, reality can only be known in signs. So great is the mystery of God, everything we know is only referential and a sign of the reality which escapes us.

Schillebeeckx, however, is suggesting that while reality is given to us by God, humans are nonetheless invited by God to give some purpose to it. "Situated within the mystery that is given to me, however, I establish a human world, the human meaning of which I am continuously changing."[60] Reality is, therefore, a mystery determined by God alone to which humanity is nonetheless invited to give meaning: "Only man can perceive meaning, but meaning is not man's creation; his mind is governed by the very 'givenness' of the world around him."[61] In a limited sense, then, humans can impose new meaning on the world. Hence, human significance or meaning is in fact an element of reality.

These same principles can also be applied to the reality of the bread and wine. Bread and wine are already the result of a human activity of giving purpose or meaning to something. They are already products of human activity insofar as meaning has been assigned to the various elements which make them up. Furthermore, this same bread and wine can be given a variety of meanings on a variety of levels apart from purely biological nourishment: "They can become the expression of fraternal solidarity, of interpersonal intimacy, of the successful conclusion of an agreement or a treaty or of the sealing of a friendship."[62] While the biological reality of the bread and wine is not denied by this further meaning, it is assumed into a higher level of meaning. And, "in that case, the bread is different because the definite relationship to man at the same time defines the reality under discussion."[63] Thus, the bread and wine, which remain bread and wine physically, are nonetheless transignified and given new meaning, new significance, by humanity.

Nevertheless, Schillebeeckx cautions:

> It should, however, be remembered that, in this case, it is a question of man's relative attitudes to the world and that the basic assumption that the being of reality is given and is, in its own being, meaningful to man remains. This preliminary and basic meaning makes man's giving of relative meanings possible and invites it.[64]

That which occurs, then, is undeniably a human recognition of the meaning of that reality which is already a given.

It is, furthermore, precisely because things have different meanings on different levels that one cannot jump from one level to another. To question whether or not the bread is actually still bread after the consecration is therefore irrelevant since it skips from the cultic, sacramental level to the physical level. And it is on this basis, then, that Schillebeeckx makes the assertion that ". . . eucharistic transubstantiation cannot be viewed in isolation from the sphere of giving meaning in sacramental signs."[65]

3. The Eucharistic Presence of Christ

Using this perception of reality as a basis, Schillebeeckx now approaches the specifically eucharistic presence of Christ. To begin, he maintains that "the basis of the entire eucharistic event is Christ's personal gift of himself to his fellow-men and, within this, to the Father."[66] The eucharist itself is but a sacramental form of Christ's self-giving. It is not, however, only the bread and wine which are the signs of that self-giving. Sacraments are never things but human actions in which matter and gesture are used to convey religious meaning. Given the Paschal context of the eucharist, "the primary sacramental form of the Eucharist is not therefore simply 'bread and wine,' but the meal in which the bread and wine are consumed."[67] The significance of the bread and wine as objects of nourishment have, therefore, been assumed into the higher function of human fellowship.[68]

The Eucharist as Meal

The understanding of the eucharist as a meal had long been neglected in Roman Catholic eucharistic theology. An over-emphasis on the presence of Christ in the elements gave rise to a limited and narrowed view of the eucharist as bread and wine. In an attempt to broaden this understanding, much greater emphasis is being given to the dynamics of the meal which becomes the sign of Christ's gift of himself. The eucharist, according to Schillebeeckx, takes on all the human significance of a meal; it is based on what humans experience when they eat a meal. To begin, a meal is not simply the eating of food, but a complex of various factors. Most people would agree that there is a vast difference between a human meal and the way in which an animal eats. Although both consist of the physical ingestion of food, the biological aspect is included and transformed in the eating together of humans in a social context:

> Between nourishment and the meal there is a difference of degree and meaning. The meal consists in eating together and following a certain order. If nourishment responds to a biological necessity, the meal responds to a properly human need. While an animal eats, a human has a meal.[69]

Sharing bread together with others in a community is an essential part of the human experience of meal. In regards to the sacrament of the eucharist, then, it is all of these elements—the total complex of the meal—which becomes the sacrament, the sign of Christ's self-giving.[70]

The Signifying Function of the Bread and Wine

Within this context, Schillebeeckx acknowledges the importance of the elements of the bread and wine which become the sign of the real presence of Christ giving himself to us:

> . . . the usual secular significance of the bread and wine is withdrawn and these become the bearers of Christ's gift of himself—"Take and eat, this is my body". . . In this commemorative meal, bread and wine become the subject of a new establishment of meaning, not by men, but by the living Lord in the Church, through which they become the sign of the real presence of Christ giving himself to us.[71]

The change which takes place is a change in the signifying function of the bread and wine. It is, therefore, a transignification which occurs. The meaning of the bread and wine, through the power of the words of consecration, are transformed to become signs through which and in which the offer of Christ's gift of himself to the Church is made, recognized and received in faith. This gift is not, however, directed towards the bread and wine, but towards the believer. Christ's presence, then, is intended for the believer, but in and by means of this gift of bread and wine.

Throughout the centuries, this notion of the bread and wine becoming signs through which the offer of Christ's gift is made has proven troublesome to eucharistic theology. The official Church has sometimes regarded the use of sign in explaining eucharistic theology with great suspicion. It would appear, however, that often this distrust of sign has been based on a false understanding of the meaning of sign. Unfortunately, sign and reality were often seen as being in opposition to each other. This opposition, however, was based on the false premise that a sign lacked real content and was only a pointer to something else which is absent. To the contrary, the term "sign" as it is used by Schillebeeckx refers to the manifestation of a distinct reality. Within the context of the eucharist, a sign is an effective sign; it ". . . does not just point to reality but realizes what it symbolizes . . . it communicates what it promised."[72] The reality is *in* the sign itself; the sign expresses the reality which is present within.

In the eucharist, the bread and wine become the signs which effect or realize the offer of Christ's presence; that is, Christ's presence exists by virtue of the fact that the bread and wine become signs: "The signifying function of the sacrament (*sacramentum est in genere signi*) is here at its highest value. It is a making present of himself of the real, living Christ in a pure, meaningful presence."[73] The use of the term "sign," then, in no way means that Christ gives something other than himself in giving this new meaning: "What is given to us in the Eucharist is nothing other than Christ himself. What the sacramental forms of bread and wine signify, and at the same time make real is not a gift that refers to Christ who gives himself in them, but Christ himself in living, personal presence."[74] This, according to Schillebeeckx, is transignification: the bread and wine are given a new meaning by Jesus, a meaning which must be recognized by humanity.

According to this understanding, the change which takes place in the eucharist is in fact an ontological change—a change in the reality of the elements. The bread is no longer bread, but at the deepest level of reality, it is the body of Christ. Outwardly, however, the physical and biological realities of the bread and wine remain intact in order to maintain their sign value: "Eucharistic sacramentality demands precisely that the physical reality does not change, otherwise there would no longer be a eucharistic sign."[75] At the deepest level of reality, however, they *are* the body and blood of

Christ. The change which occurs, then, must be understood within the sacramental framework: "the conversion is sacramental and, within this framework, it is ontological."[76]

Reciprocity: The Real Presence of Christ in the Church

A fundamental dimension of the eucharist is the bond that exists between the real presence of Christ in the eucharist and his real presence in the Church. The presence of Christ in the eucharist cannot, Schillebeeckx insists, be understood apart from the larger presence of Christ in the community: "This establishment of meaning by Christ is accomplished in the Church and thus presupposes the real presence of the Lord in the church, in the assembled community of believers and in the one who officiates at the Eucharist."[77] The celebration of the eucharist begins with a real presence of Christ and aims at making this presence more specific and intimate for the members of the community. This intimacy is the very purpose of the eucharist. As a result, the emphasis is no longer centered exclusively in the elements of bread and wine, but is expanded to include the larger sphere of the whole believing community. In fact, this is true to such an extent that if the larger presence of Christ is not considered, ". . . then the reality of Christ's presence in the Eucharist is in danger of being emptied of meaning."[78] The presence of Christ in the community is, therefore, central to the new eucharistic theology.

In keeping with the dynamics of interpersonal relationships, Schillebeeckx maintains that the believing response of the community is necessary for the complete realization of the real presence of Christ in the eucharist. The real presence in the sacrament is reciprocated when the Church makes herself present and responds by giving of self to humanity through fraternal love and service. This reciprocity, furthermore, is also signified and effected in the sacramental form of the eucharistic meal. That is, the same eucharistic species which signify sacramentally Christ's gift of self also signify and realize the Church's responding gift of faith and worship. Thus:

> The sacramental bread and wine are therefore not only the sign which makes Christ's presence real to us, but also the sign bringing about the real presence of the church (and, in the church, of us too) to him. The eu-

charistic meal thus signifies both Christ's gift of himself and the Church's responding gift of herself, of the Church who is what she is in him and can give what she gives in and through him.[79]

The real presence of Christ in the sacrament is reciprocated by the faith of the church which makes herself present with Christ.

This whole notion of reciprocity is not, however, meant to imply that the presence of Christ in the eucharist is dependent on faith. The presence of Christ, Schillebeeckx explains, is always an offered reality: "my disbelief cannot nullify the reality of Christ's real offer and the reality of the Church's remaining in Christ."[80] The real presence is really an offer of Christ's self-giving, which remains independent of faith. Nonetheless, because of the reciprocal nature of the sacrament:

the eucharistic real presence . . . is completely realized only when consent is given in faith to the eucharistic event and when this event is at the same time accomplished personally, that is, when this reciprocity takes place, in accordance with the true meaning of the sign, in the sacramental meal.[81]

The eucharistic presence of Christ reaches its full completion only when it is both offered and accepted in faith. Only then does it become the presence of Christ in the believer's heart, thus realizing the intimacy which is the purpose of the eucharist. The eucharistic reality, therefore, can only be approached by faith; to the unbeliever, that reality does not exist.

Schillebeeckx adds, however, that the reality of Christ's presence in the eucharist is always assured by virtue of the reciprocation of the believing Church. The Church, in which Christ is already present, responds in faith to Christ's offer. This response, Schillebeeckx indicates, ". . . implies a 'human' giving of meaning which does not, however, come from man, but from the Lord living in the Church or from the Church as living in the Lord."[82] Christ's presence in the Church both assures and is assured by the reciprocal response in faith which is expressed in the Church's celebration of the eucharist. The eucharistic liturgy itself is the means by which the Church responds in recognition of the establishment of the new significance of the bread and wine. And, finally, it is within this context of the community celebration that each individual responds in faith to Christ's offer. Thus, what the faith of the Church ". . . realizes in the coming about of Christ's eucharistic presence as a sacramental offer, the faith of the individual realizes in his personal acceptance of this offered presence."[83]

4. Transubstantiation and/or Transignification?

Schillebeeckx' treatise on the eucharist inevitably leads to the question of whether or not transignification is identical to, or a consequence of, transubstantiation. He begins by re-emphasizing that reality is a gift given by God and cannot, therefore, be traced back to a human giving of meaning. "It is," he explains, "only within this already given mystery, and only if man builds upon the inviolable but mysterious gift which the 'world of God' is, that man, giving meaning, can make a human world for himself."[84]

This same assertion applies to the eucharist: "The active giving of meaning in faith by the Church and with her, by the individual believer takes place within the mystery of grace of the really present 'body of the Lord' offered by God and attained by the Christian intention to reach reality."[85] On the basis of the given reality of Christ's body already present in the eucharist, the Church and the individual can both give meaning in faith to, and reach the reality of, Christ's offer. Transubstantiation, which assures that an objective reality is contained *in* the elements, necessarily precedes transignification, which asserts that a change in the signifying function of the elements has taken place.[86] The significance changes, then, because the reality has already changed.

In answer to the question of whether or not transignification and transubstantiation are identical, Schillebeeckx maintains that, while they are intimately connected they cannot simply be identified. Transignification is not simply a modernization that can be used to replace transubstantiation; to suggest that it is to change, rather than enhance, the doctrine defined at Trent and required of a believing Catholic.[87] Nor, however, does transignification deny or contradict transubstantiation. Rather, transignification, while helping to explain transubstantiation, both presupposes and demands it as a necessary element. Transubstantiation, which Christ does to the elements, is necessary for transignification, which is what humans do in recognizing the changed meaning of the elements, to occur. Peter Beer aptly sums up Schillebeeckx' thought:

> Schillebeeckx wants to be clear about this: that Christ offering himself as food and the believer receiving him as food, presupposes Christ's presence as a metaphysical priority to the believer's act of faith. Christ's real eucharistic presence does not result from man's handiwork or from man's giving of meaning alone, even if this happens within faith.[88]

It is this conclusion which is the most problematic aspect of Schillebeeckx' eucharistic theology. Jill Raitt charges that, by distinguishing between the meaning of the symbolic act and the ontological change, Schillebeeckx has restricted the fundamental idea of transignification to such an extent that it becomes insufficient. By insisting that the change which is effected by Christ must serve as the basis for the change of the meaning of this symbolic act, Raitt claims that Schillebeeckx is in effect declaring that a change in sign alone is not enough:

> . . . he has to change the fundamental idea of transignification to make it insufficient, i.e., he has to reduce it to the merely human giving of meaning whereas the change is in fact a liturgical one which involves primarily the institution of the action by Christ in the Church.[89]

According to Raitt, then, Schillebeeckx has compromised the meaning of transignification by not insisting on the reality of Christ *in* the symbolic act.

In light of Raitt's convincing argument, it is difficult not to agree with her fundamental thesis that Schillebeeckx does to some extent compromise the idea of transignification. By distinguishing between ontological and symbolic reality, it would seem that Schillebeeckx is in fact declaring that a change in sign, while important, is not significant enough to constitute the change in reality demanded by the believing Roman Catholic.

This is not just cause, however, for an overall dissatisfaction with Schillebeeckx' conclusion. Schillebeeckx, I would suggest, understands reinterpretation as an enhancement of and an addition to the traditional concept of transubstantiation rather than a total elimination of the concept. While it is undeniable that he could have stated this more clearly from the beginning, it is plausible to argue that his intent all along was to use transignification not to replace transubstantiation, but to enhance that part of transubstantiation—the personal, human dimension—which for so long had been neglected. In so doing, Schillebeeckx achieves his larger aim which was:

> . . . to interpret the reality of faith of the distinctive real presence of Christ in the Eucharist in a manner that is open to the experience of modern man and above all as an authentic Catholic dogma which every Catholic can accept and with which he can feel at home even in the new climate of thought of the twentieth century.[90]

Despite some inherent difficulties that still need to be worked out, there is much to be said for Schillebeeckx' development of eucharistic theology. It has broadened the understanding of the real presence into the context of the total sacramental act rather than in the elements alone. His development of transignification places the statement of transubstantiation in its religious context and removes the change in the substance of the bread into the substance of the body of Christ from a merely physical level to a specifically sacramental level.[91] In using transignification to enhance transubstantiation, Schillebeeckx indicates that the notion of a change occurring at the eucharist is no longer simply a matter of physical change, but also a matter of a change in the meaning and significance of the elements of the bread and wine for the believer and the larger Church. As a result, the emphasis has been returned from the elements to the effect on the people. The intimate relationship with Christ which is the *purpose* of the real presence is given priority over the fact of the real presence. It is, therefore, to the credit of transignification that the eucharistic conversion is moving from the objective categories to more personal, human categories of meaning and significance. By moving the eucharistic change from the objective level to a more subjective, sacramental level, Schillebeeckx is attempting to deepen the meaning of transubstantiation and thus make it more relevant to those participating in the eucharist. Hence, as Marie Zimmerman concludes: "Ainsi donc, si la transsignification nécessite la réalité exprimée par la transsubstantiation, cette première évite de situer la derniére au plan de l'objectivation, car dans le domaine de la physique, la transsubstantiation reste sans signification."[92]

Conclusion: Vatican Response

On September 3, 1965, Pope Paul VI issued the encyclical *Mysterium Fidei* to the "patriarchs, primates, archbishops, bishops, and other local ordinaries . . . and to the clergy and faithful of the entire world."[93] Although Paul VI never specifically mentions anyone by name, many sources (especially in the Italian press) cited Dutch Catholic theologians as being those to whom the encyclical was directed. "They call attention to the fact that almost the only known Catholic advocacy of new speculative views on the Eucharist in recent years has come from a few Dutch thinkers."[94] In reply, *Osservatore Romano* published a statement, ". . . saying that the encyclical was not directed against the clergy of any country in particular."[95] Nevertheless, most commentators on the encyclical agree that it must have been directed at least in part to the theology which was emerging from the Netherlands.

Indeed, as Rene Marle points out,

> s'il ne s'était agi que de la Hollande, on voit mal pourquoi le Souverain Pontife, si soucieux de manifester la confiance qu'il porte à l'épiscopat, aurait éprouvé le besoin d'intervenir en quelque sorte pardessus la tête des évêques ou de porter devant l'Eglise universelle les conflits et misères affectant uniquement une communauté particulière.[96]

Despite the fact that the person or persons to whom the encyclical is directed remains unclear, the purpose and scope of it is obvious:

> . . . some of those who are dealing with this Most Holy Mystery in speech and writing are disseminating opinions on Masses celebrated in private or on the dogma of

transubstantiation that are disturbing the minds of the faithful and causing them no small measure of confusion about matters of faith.[97]

Paul VI is concerned that some misrepresentation and misunderstanding could and has occurred among both the faithful and priests who do not correctly understand the new theology. Hence, "the Pope's preoccupation seems to be to reassure the faithful; at the same time he warns the serious theologian of the dangers of misunderstanding by those less well equipped to appreciate the nuances of theological meaning."[98]

Despite this seeming condemnation, however, Paul VI adamantly denies that he disapproves of or wishes to hamper theological renewal in the field of the eucharist. Rather, he commends the ". . . praiseworthy effort to investigate this lofty Mystery and to set forth its inexhaustible riches and to make it more understandable to the men of today; rather, We acknowledge this and We approve of it."[99] It is clear that he is not condemning theological speculation about the eucharist. He does, however, insist that any attempts at reinterpretation must maintain the teaching of the past: ". . . he is insisting that such growth be consonant with the traditional faith of the Church so that, in the progress of the understanding of our faith, the unchangeable truth of faith be maintained."[100]

While commending the effort that has been made in making the eucharist more understandable to the contemporary person, Paul VI does delineate four deviations from the teaching and practice of the Church which must be condemned:

> 1. Extolling the "community" mass in a way that detracts from Masses that are celebrated privately; 2. Concentrating on the notion of sacramental sign as if the symbol fully expresses the manner of Christ's presence; 3. Neglecting the Council of Trent's teaching on transubstantiation to the extent that the body and blood of Christ involve merely a "transignification"or "transfinalization" and nothing more; 4. Proposing or acting as if Christ is no longer present in the consecrated hosts after the celebration of the Mass.[101]

Although other aspects of eucharistic doctrine are brought to surface in the encyclical (in particular the private masses and the adoration of the Eucharist), most notable is the emphasis that is put on preserving the doctrine of the real presence of Christ in the eucharist and the dogma of transubstantiation. "Le plus important de ces gauchissements ou appauvrissements," maintains Marle, "est sans doute celui qui concerne la présence réele et le dogme de la "transsubstantiation."[102]

In accord with the teaching of Vatican II, Paul VI begins, not by concentrating on the eucharistic presence, but by affirming the different modes of Christ's presence in the Church: in the prayers, the works of mercy, the preaching, the ruling of the Church as well as in the sacrifice of the Mass and the administration of the sacraments. All of these, however, are surpassed by Christ's substantial presence in the eucharist. "This presence," explains the encyclical, "is called 'real' not to exclude the idea that the others are 'real' too, but rather to indicate presence *par excellence*, because it is substantial and through it Christ becomes present whole and entire, God and man."[103]

Symbolism, according to Paul VI, while important, is inadequate to express this real presence of Christ in the eucharist: "It does not indicate or explain what it is that makes this Sacrament different from all the others."[104] Instead, that which is necessary to express the real presence is the Tridentine dogma of transubstantiation, which "assures us that the way in which Christ becomes present in this sacrament is through the conversion of the whole substance of the bread into His body and of the whole substance of the wine into His blood . . ."[105] The encyclical, then, is directed against any theory which would remove the idea of a substantial change in the eucharist and which is expressed by transubstantiation. Accordingly, any attempt

> . . . to discuss the mystery of transubstantiation without mentioning what the Council of Trent had to say about the marvelous conversion of the whole substance of the bread into the Body and the whole substance of the wine into the blood of Christ, as if they involve nothing more that "transignification," or "transfinalization" as they call it . . .[106]

is insufficient.

Nonetheless, as many proponents of the new eucharistic theology assert, Paul VI does not outrightly condemn transignification or transfinalization. Rather, he insists that the eucharistic change cannot be thought of only in these terms nor apart from the ontological change which is expressed by transubstantiation:

> As a result of transubstantiation, the species of bread and wine undoubtedly take on a new signification and a new finality, for they are no longer ordinary bread but instead a sign of something sacred and a sign of spiritual food; but they take on this new signification, this new finality, precisely because they contain a new "reality" which we can rightly call ontological.[107]

Once transubstantiation does occur, the bread and wine do indeed, Paul VI affirms, take on a new meaning and a new finality, but only as a result of the new ontological reality which they now contain. The transignification and the transfinalization which occur are, then, a consequence of transubstantiation. Thus, "what is condemned then is not transignification and transfinalization as such, but the reduction of transubstantiation to these and nothing more."[108]

In the final analysis, there does not seem to be much difference between that which Schillebeeckx proposes in *The Eucharist* and that which is outlined in *Mysterium Fidei*. While it is true that at first glance the encyclical does appear to be an outright condemnation of transignification, this is not the case.[109] Rather, both Schillebeeckx and Paul VI arrive at the same basic conclusion: transignification does in fact occur but cannot be thought of apart from transubstantiation. Perhaps, as Paul Jersild suggests, Schillebeeckx' final conclusion was in part ". . . motivated by criticism of the new eucharistic theology from within his church . . ."[110] Be that as it may, however, it is worth reiterating that, despite certain weaknesses, Schillebeeckx does accomplish that which he sets out to do. By emphasizing the importance of transignification in the eucharistic change, he does in fact put the eucharist in the more subjective and personal realm of human meaning and significance and, in so doing, makes it more relevant to the twentieth century person. While safeguarding the traditional doctrine expressed at Trent and, at the same time, staying within the bounds of orthodoxy, Schillebeeckx manages to both clarify and deepen the meaning of transubstantiation in order that the twentieth century person ". . . might live it in a more authentic fashion and, so to speak, in a more existential manner."[111]

Discussion Questions

1. What factors influenced the shift in emphasis in Roman Catholic eucharistic theology?

2. What is meant by Jesus as the primordial sacrament? Church as a basic sacrament? Explain.

3. What is the difference between the earlier understanding of sacrament and the understanding that began to be developed in the late 1950's and the early 1960's?

4. How does the new framework in which Schillebeeckx' eucharistic theology is situated differ from the old?

5. How does Schillebeeckx' emphasis on the meal aspect of the eucharist differ from the pre-Vatican II understanding of the eucharist?

6. As Schillebeeckx uses it, what does the term "sign" mean in reference to eucharist?

7. What does Schillebeeckx mean by "reciprocity"? How does this differ from a pre-Vatican II understanding of the eucharist? Explain.

8. How does Schillebeeckx explain the relationship between transignification and transubstantiation? What is the difficulty with his explanation?

9. What helpful dimensions has Schillebeeckx' reinterpretation of the eucharist added to Roman Catholic eucharistic theology? In other words, in what ways does Schillebeeckx' perception of the eucharist help make it more relevant for the twentieth century person?

10. What aspects of Schillebeeckx' eucharistic theology does Rome find unacceptable? Do you agree?

11. What dimensions of Schillebeeckx theology do you find most helpful to your own personal understanding of the eucharist? Explain.

Chapter Four

The Eucharist—A Sacrament of Service

WITHIN THE LAST THREE DECADES A NEW PHENOMENON has arisen on the theological scene: liberation theology. Throughout the years, the impact of the theology of liberation has gone far from being merely a Latin American concern; it is now in *the* forefront of theological reflection and has even gone beyond the borders of the Church to become of interest to the general public.[1] It is within this context of liberation theology, furthermore, that a new eucharistic theology is being developed. Liberation theologians, who also recognize the need to make the doctrine of the eucharist relevant for the layperson of the twentieth century, are going beyond this need for relevancy to reach out to those who are in, or concerned with, a situation of oppression and injustice. The meaning of the eucharist, they claim, is that of service. The eucharist *must* be understood as a consciousness-raising, community-forming event in which service and liberation are the main focus and outcome. The social dimension of the eucharist is foremost.

Liberation Theology

1. The History and Development of Liberation Theology

The roots of contemporary liberation theology are most definitely based in Latin America. Although precursors of this type of theology can be traced back to the earliest colonial days in Latin America, it was not until the 1960's that a concrete theology of liberation emerged on the scene.[2] Thus it was that during the 1960's, Latin American theologians began to make a break away from European theology and to take Latin America as their context for study.[3]

Two factors in particular led to the creation of liberation theology. First, the 1960's were a time of socio-political unrest in many Latin American countries. The recognition that many governments advocated a form of development which benefited only the rich and excluded the majority of the population gave rise to popular movements seeking change in socio-economic structures. Latin Americans became aware that Western achievements should not be taken as the norm and, moreover. that the development of the Western world had occurred at the expense of the Third World.[4] The developmentalist theory which implied that underdeveloped countries must catch up to developed countries by imitation was henceforth rejected. Instead, the understanding grew that "if the underdeveloped countries are to attain liberation, they must break the cycle of dependence on the advanced, industrialized countries."[5] The existing social structures were therefore called into question. This, in turn, aided in the development of liberation theology.[6]

Along with the socio-political factor, there was also a distinct ecclesial factor that helped give rise to the development of liberation theology. Of primary importance was the Second

Vatican Council with its emphasis on freedom and creativity in theology. It was as a result of this freedom that the Latin American church in particular began to understand itself as a pilgrim church and human history as the place in which God is at work. As a result of Vatican II, then, the Church was ". . . led to a profound re-evaluation of its mission in the world and of the understanding of the Christian message."[7] The conference of 1968 at Medellin further developed this understanding. By officially applying the concepts of Vatican II to Latin America, Medellin gave the new theology of the Council concrete form in Latin America.[8] It was, therefore, a combination of political and religious factors which precipitated the concretization of liberation theology: "In the 1960's new questions about the social order urgently demanded new answers, and church people felt a new freedom to respond."[9]

Of course, liberation theology is no longer a purely Latin American phenomenon. It is, rather, ". . . a product of the Third World, enunciated thus far most clearly in Latin America, but with significant parallels among the dispossessed elsewhere (blacks in North America, Africa and Asia, for e.g.) . . ."[10] Latin American liberation theology is but one aspect, albeit the most prominent, of a much larger movement.

As a result of the growth of the movement in various countries, liberation theology is becoming increasingly diversified. Insofar as different countries have different concerns, the emphases developed in liberation theology are widely varied. The major concern in Latin American liberation theology, for example, is the socio-economically poor; those who, according to Leonardo Boff, lack or are deprived of the necessary means by which to live.[11] This type of material poverty is looked upon as an evil which dehumanizes people. It is, therefore, contrary to the will of God and something from which people should seek to be liberated.[12] The theology of liberation that is being developed in Asia, on the other hand, is distinct from Latin American theology insofar as it focuses mainly on inculturation. It seeks to recognize Christ's presence in non-Christian religions in order to enter into meaningful dialogue with them. Dialogue is not, however, the only objective. Instead, this dialogue is established primarily ". . . with a view to awakening their huge potential for social liberation."[13]

Hence both the inculturationist and the liberationist approaches are present in Asian liberation theology.

African liberation theology, too, shows aspects of both approaches. On the one hand, African liberation theologians are striving to reclaim the African culture and religious traditions which were ignored or destroyed during colonization. At times, this inculturationist approach comes into conflict with South African black theology which insists that liberation theology must go beyond the rehabilitation of African traditions to be a prophetic voice for the poor and oppressed.[14] To suggest, however, that these two approaches are in constant conflict is incorrect. To the contrary, the inculturationist approach is often ". . . liberating insofar as it amounts to affirming their own being as Asians and Africans."[15] Thus, despite the vast differences in the expressions of liberation theology that are found on the different continents, all have much the same goal, although it may be approached in different ways. All are concerned with the liberation of those who suffer from any kind of oppression, be it social, economic, political, religious or racial.

2. Toward a Definition of Liberation Theology

It would be appropriate at this point, after having traced the history and development of liberation theology, to give a definition of this new type of theology. Liberation theology, according to Clodovis Boff, is "faith reflection on the praxis of liberation" or, in other words, "reflection on the life of the Christian community from a standpoint of its contribution to liberation."[16] Such a definition, however, should not lead one to believe that reflection alone is the most important element in liberation theology. To the contrary, liberation theologians insist that the primary concern is the *action* of liberating those who are oppressed within human history. Hence, liberation theology is ". . . not so much a new theme for reflection as a new way to do theology . . . This is a theology which does not stop with reflecting on the world, but rather tries to be part of the process through which the world is transformed."[17]

Liberation theology marks a break away from a purely academic form of theology.[18] Liberation theologians do not, for the most part, teach full-time at a university, but spend a good portion of their time with grassroots communities, contributing to the community the benefits of an academic education. In fact, Gutierrez even goes so far as to claim that it is precisely because of this contact that the theologians are in fact theologians: ". . . professional theologians must be linked with a Christian community in order to gain answers."[19] As a result, liberation theologians are developing a theology that is truly from the people.

The primary element, or first act, of liberation theology is not the theology itself. It is, rather, a commitment to the oppressed and their struggle for liberation.[20] In order for this commitment to occur, direct, personal contact with the oppressed is a necessary pre-condition. By listening directly to the experiences of the people and observing their actions, one begins to recognize the presence of God in their suffering and struggle. From this recognition comes the conversion of lifestyle.[21] Jose Miguez-Bonino describes this conversion as follows: ". . . what is needed is transformation—the kind of understanding that penetrates beyond facts to reality, the kind of understanding that can change lives."[22] Once transformation occurs, true commitment to the poor can and does take place.

It is only after taking this first step of making a commitment that the secondary element—critical reflection—can occur: the ". . . commitment of faith precedes the origin of any theological reflection."[23] Once the action is committed, reflection on that action can take place. Liberation theology is, therefore, a reflection on what has transpired as a result of the first act of commitment and as such is most definitely the second act.

3. The Methodology of Liberation Theology

Social Analysis

The methodology of this critical reflection on praxis (or theology) occurs in three stages. First, social analysis must happen. Theologians must inform themselves about the forms of oppression that are suffered and, in so doing, discover the reasons and causes of that oppression. In Latin America, for example, where the pre-dominant expression of oppression is socio-economic poverty, theologians have determined that poverty occurs as a result of unjust social structures and plunder by oppressors. The way to end such oppression, they have concluded, is to transform or replace the existing social structures with alternatives.[24]

Liberation theology uses a different set of tools than does classical theology. Whereas in the past, philosophy was used as an aid to theology (e.g. Aquinas' use of Aristotle), liberation theology is using the social sciences—more specifically, sociology and political science—as an aid.[25] Marxism in particular is especially useful for liberation theologians as an instrument for social analysis. This is not to imply, of course, that liberation theology is based on Marxism or that those involved with the struggle for liberation are Marxists. To the contrary, most liberation theologians hasten to insist that ". . . the Bible provides our overall approach to life, while Marx is simply a useful analytical tool."[26]

Hermeneutical Meditation

The second step after having analyzed the social conditions is hermeneutical meditation. In this step, the Bible (and often church documents) is re-read from the perspective of the oppressed and in terms of their own experience.[27] The important element in this re-reading of the Bible is not to interpret Scripture, but to interpret their own experience in light of the Scriptures. Application of Bible texts to daily life is, therefore, an important component of doing theology.

The major themes with which liberation theology deals most often come from this type of re-reading of the Bible. For example, from the story of Exodus comes the conviction that God does indeed side with the oppressed. By reading the Exodus account, those who are oppressed today come to the realization that God is concerned with the quality of social, political and economic structures, and that liberation from these unjust structures can be, as it was for the Hebrews, the basis for the religious experience of liberation from sin.[28]

Likewise, when re-reading the Gospel accounts from their own situation of oppression, liberation theologians have developed a new christology. Without making Jesus out to be a social revolutionary, they have put the emphasis on Jesus' humanity, with all of its social and political implications. As a result, they are able to point out the similarities between their own and Jesus' situation as well as to demonstrate Jesus' liberative program and practices.[29]

Stemming from such a christology is the conviction that God reveals Himself in human history, and that the Kingdom which Jesus preached is not in another world, but a transformation of this one. "We must," according to Enrique Dussel, "come to realize that day-to-day history is the one and only place where God reveals himself to us . . . God reveals himself before our eyes in our neighbor and in history."[30] The concern of liberation theology is not, therefore, with an interior or otherworldly spirituality. Rather, the focus is with this world and God's revelation of the Kingdom on earth.

Practical Mediation

After re-reading the Bible in light of one's own situation, the final stage in doing liberation theology is practical mediation. At this point, people combine the knowledge gained from the first two stages in order to work out a plan of action. During this period a decision is made regarding what is possible, strategy and tactics are defined and a program for action is drawn up.[31] Hence, liberation theology both begins and ends with action: "theology must both issue from engagement and lead to renewed engagement."[32] It is, therefore, a theology which keeps in tension both theory and practice.[33]

4. Levels of Liberation Theology

Liberation theology is not only the task of professional theologians. There are, in fact, three integrated levels at which liberation theology is done: professional, pastoral and popular. The theology which is done at these three levels is substantially the same; that which makes them distinct is the language which is used at each level.[34] At the professional level are those professional theologians who have spent years in study, writing and teaching, but who are nonetheless an integral part of the community. In addition, liberation theology is lived at the pastoral level by those pastors, sisters and lay people who are committed to liberation. At this level, liberation theology enters into the fields of catechesis, liturgy, spirituality, art and preaching. The third level—the popular level—is the most important level according to Boff since it is the one at which liberation theology is most present and alive.[35] The people at this level include all those characterized by lack of employment, housing, food, health and education.[36] They are, therefore, those who live within the situation of oppression and are seeking concrete liberation from it. It is these people, then, who make up the basic Christian communities.

5. Basic Christian Communities

Basic Christian communities are ". . . small lay-led communities, motivated by Christian faith, that see themselves as part of the church and that are committed to working together to improve their communities and to establish a more just society."[37] They are, most liberation theologians agree, *the* primary embodiment of liberation theology and, some would say, of the wider church. Enrique Dussel, for example, emphatically declares: "I would say that we cannot really be part of the living Church nowadays without being a member of such a community."[38] Basic Christian communities, therefore, without being a parallel Church, are most definitely a new form of being church within the larger church society. As such, they seek to bridge the gap between the impersonal, hierarchical church and the individuals who are part of it.[39]

The reasons for the emergence of these base Christian communities in the late 1960's are numerous. First, previous experiences with small groups such as Curcillo or Catholic Action where the small cell structure was basic to the group served as an early antecedent to the basic Christian communities.[40] More importantly, the awareness that the existing system of huge parishes was largely inappropriate for countries where people were widely dispersed led to the recognition that smaller, closer groups were necessary. Likewise, there ensued a growing desire for a distinctly Latin American form of church which would involve a larger number of people.[41] Furthermore, the acute shortage of priests in these countries has necessarily meant an increased role for the laity:

> The rise of the basic communities is also due to the crisis in the church institution. The scarcity of ordained ministers to attend to the needs of these communities has aroused the creative imagination of the pastors themselves, and they have come to entrust the laity with more and more responsibility.[42]

The basic Christian communities are, therefore, by and large a lay movement. While it is true that a great number of the communities got their start from a priest or sister, it is nonetheless the lay people who are in charge of the community and its ministries. Lay participation is primary and occurs to such an extent that it is no longer only priests and sisters who are starting the communities, but lay people from other communities. Lay participation, then, is developing more and more into lay leadership.[43]

Basic Christian communities are essentially pastoral. The oppressed meet together to try to understand their situation and the problems arising from it in the light of the Bible and their own faith. They then seek to remedy those problems by obtaining the services and resources that they deem necessary.[44]

As a result of the way in which they seek to remedy these problems, however, the communities also have a tremendous social and political impact. The process of conscientization—through which community members first try to discover the cause of their oppression and then organize themselves into movements which will take direct action in solving the problem—cannot help but have a profound bearing on the social and political environments. Furthermore, because of the action which the communities take, they are often bound up with the popular movement, which includes all organizations and activities by which the oppressed manifest their struggle for liberation. While the popular movement does add an extra dimension of strength to the communities, that which the communities give to the popular movement is more important: a testimony to the God who is working with the poor in their struggle for liberation.[45]

Theology of the Sacraments in Liberation Theology

Liberation theology has had and continues to have an influence in *all* realms of theology. The theology of the sacraments, for example, undergoes a substantial change in emphasis when considered from within the framework of liberation theology. While affirming the accomplishments of Schillebeeckx and Rahner which perceive the sacraments as personal, saving encounters between God and humanity, liberation theologians such as Juan Luis Segundo are placing much more emphasis on an equally important dimension of the sacraments: the community.[46]

The starting point for Segundo is his conviction that the meaning behind the sacraments has been distorted through the centuries. This crisis of meaning is due in large part to the fact that the sacraments are often understood as magical actions:

Magical actions are different from ordinary actions in two respects . . . Firstly, in terms of expected efficacy, there is no normal relationship between the means employed and the outcome. Secondly, the outcome is not dependent on whim; it is tied by a superhuman power to fixed ritual gestures or words.[47]

When sacraments are understood as actions which produce grace as long as the proper rite is performed (with the minimum human disposition), a magical conception of the sacraments is understandable. The tendency to interpret the sacraments in terms of their efficacy alone gives them a magical orientation. Moreover, in line with this understanding, that which is considered the most important is the grace which is accumulated by partaking in these magical rites. Thus, ". . . there is no doubt that the common sacramental theology is of the 'bank deposit' type."[48]

The basis of this magic-oriented sacramental theology is the dualism that exists between everyday life and religious life, between the sacred and the profane: "we find a conflict between the 'religious' conception of Christianity and their real life experience of a desacralized world."[49] A magical view of the sacraments occurs when God's activity is limited to certain rites which effect salvation in religious life, *independent* of that which occurs in history: "Magic is a matter of looking for divine efficacy in certain procedures without any relation to historical efficacy."[50] When God's activity is limited to otherworldly activities, rather than those in human history, the meaning of the sacraments becomes distorted.

Segundo contends that this crisis which is occurring is not simply a crisis of the sacraments, but, more fundamentally, a crisis of the Christian community:

> In short, what is plaguing us is not a crisis over the sacraments but a crisis over the coherence and meaningfulness of the Christian community. There are times when it seems that our yearning and zeal for ritual reform and liturgical renewal is a superficial way of solving a much deeper problem. For it enables us to hide from the real problem: the problem of community.[51]

The more profound problem rests, therefore, with the meaninglessness of the Christian community in the present day situation.

When the Christian community is deemed valuable simply because it dispenses the sacraments, it too becomes magical and otherworldly, and bears little relationship to human history. To the contrary, the community must be historically realistic; its members must be concerned with each other and with this world. It must be a community in the truest sense of the word:

> . . . it must be a community of mutual aid in which people practice the dimensions of real encounter and fraternal love, not simply by reading or reflection, but by proffering real, concrete help . . . The community ought to be able to free itself on every level (material, moral, etc.) so that it can exercise service to the rest of mankind.[52]

And, as this type of community, the Christian community would itself be transformed into a sacrament and sign of salvation.

The true meaning of the sacraments can be brought to light by a correct understanding of what the Christian community can and should be. Rather than the importance of the sacraments being attributed to the grace conferred on the individual, a new understanding of the sacraments would see the efficacy in their ability to aid in the community forming process. Hence, the sacraments

> . . . are made so that the grace conferred may structure a community by way of signification; so that it may be turned into a community; and even more specifically, so that it may be turned into a community that thinks and dialogues in terms of what is really taking place in history, above and beyond mere appearance.[53]

Thus, the efficacy of the sacraments should be dependent on their ability to help create a community which is true to its call of service. As a result, they should no longer be understood as rites which ensure individual salvation. Rather, the sacraments must become signs which promote the liberation of the entire community. The grace which is received in the sacraments is, therefore, the grace that will prepare the community to be a liberating factor in history.

Finally, it should be pointed out that an understanding of the sacraments as community-building events will undoubtedly lead to the desacralization of the priesthood. This interpretation no longer professes that the grace of the sacrament is received only through the performance of sacred rites. Rather, the entire community is itself grace-filled. As a result, the conception of the minister of the sacraments will necessarily change: "So long as the priest's functions were seen by the faithful as something which had direct, salvific value, things that had efficacy in themselves independently of their benefit to the rest of mankind, then the priest himself felt he had a definite place in society."[54] With the modified understanding of the sacraments, this perception of the priest will also be altered. The priest's role will be one of service: the minister who serves the community in their historical struggle. Thus, the sacraments will become truly *for* the people; instead of being solely the possession of the priest, the sacraments will be given back to the community.

The Re-interpretation of the Eucharist in Liberation Theology

As with most facets of Christian theology, liberation theologians are striving to re-interpret the doctrine of the eucharist from within the context of the struggle for liberation. Due to the centrality of the eucharist to Roman Catholicism, it is inconceivable that the doctrine of the eucharist would remain untouched by a new way of doing theology which is giving a total re-orientation to Christianity. It is important to recognize, however, that the eucharist is not one of the foremost concerns to liberation theologians. The document on liturgy, which was given first place at the Second Vatican Council, was given ninth position at Medellin. This is a good indication that the primary focus of liberation theology is not with doctrine, but with the human situation in which that doctrine is encountered.[55]

Furthermore, liberation theology is a relatively new way of doing theology. It is not surprising, therefore, that not all aspects of Christian theology have been completely developed within the new framework. Dermot Lane confirms this: "One particular area in which the perspectives of political theology, liberation theology and social theology have yet to be fully applied is the liturgy of the eucharist."[56] Hence, it is *not* a fully developed theology of the eucharist which has emerged from liberation theology. Be this as it may, however, theologians such as Tissa Balasuriya and Leonardo Boff (to name but two) have come to the conclusion that a re-interpretation of the eucharist is a necessary component of the overall re-orientation of theology.

1. The Irrelevance and Meaninglessness of the Eucharistic Celebration

In agreement with many other theologians both during and since the Second Vatican Council, the majority of liberation theologians are convinced that the eucharist as it is understood and practised in the present day is, at least to some extent, lacking in relevance for those who partake of it:

> That so-called sacrament as it is celebrated in our churches has little or no relevance for modern [people], precisely because it has little or nothing to do with eating and drinking outside church walls. It has nothing to do with the problems of poverty and hunger which oppress all people in their daily lives. The Lord's Supper has no relation to their work, their economics and their politics.[57]

The eucharist as it is now being celebrated seems to have little relation to the social issues of the day. It is often seen as an otherworldly flight from the problems of this world into an individualistic, pietistic world: "liturgy provides something of 'a break' from the hurly-burly of daily life and 'an escape' from the social responsibilities we bear for the world around us."[58]

This lack of relevance, however, would seem to stem from a deeper problem: the lack of *meaning* in the celebration of the eucharist. "There have," Tissa Balasuriya argues, "been serious distortions in its meaning. Whereas it began with the sacrifice of self for the liberation of others, it has long been a means of enslavement and domestication of believers."[59] The true inner meaning of the eucharist has been changed and often obliterated. Too often, the eucharist has become a means of perpetuating injustice both by forcing the oppressed to accept their condition for the sake of unity and by legitimizing the oppressors' activities of exploitation. During the colonization of the Americas and Asia, for example, "the Eucharist went side by side with the worst and largest-scale exploitation that the world has ever seen . . . It has evolved alongside the world's worst exploitation and did not contest it or, rather, it tended to justify the status quo."[60]

As a result of the irrelevance and meaninglessness of the eucharist, the Christian community has broken down. Those who oppose what the eucharist has become and what it supports no longer have their needs fulfilled at a standard celebration of the eucharist and therefore no longer attend. "It is not uncommon to find Christians fully committed to the creation of a better world for the sake of the Kingdom of God, who have at the same time opted out of the eucharistic community."[61] These people will move away from the large-scale celebration of the Mass to small group celebrations or prayer meetings or paraliturgies. It is these same people, moreover, who are in the process of renewing the eucharist so that its meaning may be restored.

2. The History of the Eucharist

Old Testament Background

The starting point in restoring the inner meaning of the eucharist within the context of liberation theology is to determine the biblical meaning of the eucharist. To begin, then, attention must be focused on the Old Testament background to the eucharist—the Jewish Passover and the Jewish prophetic tradition—as the context within which Jesus instituted the eucharist. For the Jews, the Passover was the national celebration of their liberation from slavery in Egypt. This liberation, which prefigured the subsequent liberation of all of humanity in Christ, was not a matter of social assistance, nor was it a situation from which people could liberate themselves merely through prayer. Rather, "the liberation which God wrought for his people was a political liberation."[62] Liberation in this case meant a physical struggle for freedom in which the people participated, but in which God was involved and fully in charge. Thus, the Passover celebrated God's concern for His people within their own human history.

The prophetic tradition is also a decisive aspect of the Old Testament background to the eucharist. Many of the prophets explicitly condemn worship without justice. Amos, for example, spurned worship which had no relation to a concern for the poor and oppressed:

I hate, I despise your feasts, and I take no delight in your solemn assemblies . . . Take away from me the noise of your songs; to the melody of your harps I will not listen. But let justice roll down like waters, and righteousness like an everflowing stream. (Amos 5:21,23-24, RSV)

Genuine worship, therefore, necessarily included a concern for others. In fact, to worship God without caring for the poor and marginalized was not to worship at all, since God had shown Himself through the Exodus to be concerned with His people: ". . . to know God is to know a God of justice. It is only with this understanding that God can be worshipped authentically."[63]

New Testament Accounts of the Eucharist

It is from within this context that Jesus based his own teachings. Like Moses of the Old Testament, Jesus found his people under the domination of oppressive foreign powers and set out to liberate them.[64] And, like the prophets, Jesus protested against wrong political and religious structures. In Matthew, for example, Jesus manifests the link between justice and worship that was evident in the prophetic tradition: "So if you are offering your gift at the altar, and there remember that your brother has something against you, leave your gift there before the altar and go; first be reconciled with your brother, and then come and offer your gift." (Matthew 5:23-24, RSV)

Moreover, from reading the Gospels, it becomes apparent that Jesus' concern throughout his entire ministry was for just relationships between humans. The parable of the rich man and Lazarus (Lk. 16:19-31) and the story of the woman caught in adultery (Jn. 16:19-31) are but two examples of this. Is it any surprise, then, that this concern for justice is carried over and made a necessary and integral part of worship? For Jesus, "one's piety ought to be the expression of a righteous and just life."[65]

When read from within the context of liberation theology, all the New Testament accounts of the eucharist seem to indicate that "for Jesus, the eucharist was primarily the supreme symbol of his self-offering unto death."[66] The eucharist was the action in which Jesus explained the significance and meaning of his life and death: the giving of self to others for the cause of total human liberation. It was the symbolic action of who Jesus was and why he became incarnate: to free those oppressed by sin and by other forms of oppression which are rooted in sin.[67] For Jesus, the eucharist which he instituted at the Last Supper was the fulfillment of the Jewish Passover which celebrated the liberation of God's people from Egypt.

In the three synoptic gospels as well as in I Corinthians, the institution of the eucharist occurs during a meal. As a result, the eucharist becomes the symbol of the equality of the participants. Gustavo Gutierrez explains this idea in these words: ". . . communion with God and others presupposes the abolition of all injustice and exploitation. This is expressed by the very fact that the eucharist was instituted during a meal. For the Jews, a meal in common was a sign of brotherhood."[68] As a meal, the eucharist points to the abolition of injustice and inequality.

Furthermore, from within this context of a meal, the emphasis of the eucharist was placed on the gesture of sharing the bread and wine: "the simple, central action of the eucharist is the sharing of food—not only the eating but the sharing."[69] It was this gesture which symbolized the whole of Jesus' life of giving to others and which also provided a way for Jesus to be present to his followers after his death:

> It was in this gesture of Jesus—in which he put his whole self because it summed up his whole life, in which everything was shared—a life totally given (even to dying for those he loved)—that his disciples were to recognize him after his resurrection; it was this gesture that summed up his last commandments to his disciples—the *mandatum*; it was through this gesture that they would celebrate him and steep themselves in his thought and his ethics.[70]

That which was of importance to Jesus, then, was the actual fact of sharing which symbolized his own sharing of himself with others.

In John's gospel, the account of the washing of the feet provides a further indication that the eucharist was for Jesus a sign of unity among humans. By his act of menial service of washing his disciples' feet, Jesus ". . . acted to abolish the inequality between them, deliberately reversing their social positions and roles" and was, therefore, "subverting in principle all structures of domination."[71] Thus, the eucharist was for Jesus a sign which implied the abrogation of injustice and domination.

More importantly, John's account of the washing of the feet gives testimony to the perception of the eucharist as a symbol of Jesus' self-giving. According to Sandra Schneiders, John's version is ". . . the analogue of the eucharistic institution narratives in the synoptic accounts of the supper, i.e., it functions as the symbol and catechesis of Jesus' approaching death, his handing over of himself for and to his disciples."[72] Insofar as it reveals Jesus' action of service for others, the washing of the feet is a reflection on the profound meaning of the eucharist. That which was most important to John was not the institution of the eucharist itself, but that for which the eucharist stood. Thus, "in replacing the liturgical act of the eucharist with the washing of the feet, John is here substituting for the sacrament the reality that it signifies, namely the active service of others in charity."[73]

Furthermore, in the account of the Last Supper in all four gospels, Jesus provides his followers with a mandate: to continue to live in the way that he had lived by giving of themselves in service to others. In the synoptics, the institution of the eucharist is followed by the command: "Do this in memory of me." "This," according to certain liberation theologians, referred in principle to the action of sharing which was symbolized in the eucharist: "The command of Jesus, "Do this," refers primarily to his giving of himself for the people, and secondarily to the ritualistic commemoration of this giving."[74] The participants at the eucharist were therefore called upon to give of themselves as Jesus had. In John's gospel, likewise, the account of the washing of feet is concluded with a command which parallels that of the institution narratives: "You should also do what I have done for you." This command was an explicit reference to the act of service which Jesus had demonstrated and an exhortation to those present to do the same.

Leonardo Boff adds an interesting dimension to the understanding of the eucharist as it is found in the four Gospel accounts. Boff indicates that the passages which carry the accounts of the Last Supper are texts which are based on the witness of a covenant community which was *already* celebrating the eucharist. The meaning which is given to the eucharist in these accounts is, therefore, the meaning which was given to it by the early Christian community. Within this context, ". . . the Last Supper appears to have had a distinctly eschatological connotation . . . as a symbol of the heavenly repast to be enjoyed in the Kingdom of God . . ."[75] In keeping with such a perception, the eucharist was also to be understood as a foreshadowing of that time when all—oppressed and oppressors without distinction—will eat the shared meal together in fellowship. The eucharist becomes not merely the memorial of the Last Supper alone, but a celebration of all those significant meals when Jesus had fed the hungry and shared meals with the tax collectors, sinners and other marginals of his society. Once again, the conclusion is obvious: those who follow Jesus must do likewise. Hence, ". . . those who celebrate the eucharist in memory of Jesus, who follow his command to "do this," must feed the same sort of people and involve themselves with the same sort of dinner guests as Christ had at table."[76]

Early Church Understanding of the Eucharist

After Jesus' death and resurrection, the early Christian community continued to celebrate the eucharist in a way that was true to its meaning. In the Acts of the Apostles, the eucharist was briefly referred to as the breaking of the bread, and was accompanied by a communal meal and fellowship. It was an informal event: "They listened to the teaching of the apostles, they prayed together, they conversed about their own problems, they shared a meal and commemorated the Lord."[77] The description of the eucharist itself in Acts was brief. However, its relation to the social lives of the participants is evident. After referring to the breaking of bread, the author of Acts continued: "And all who believed were together, and had all things in common; and they sold their possessions and goods and distributed them to all, as any had need." (Acts

2:44-45, RSV) According to certain liberation theologians, this explicit concern for others took place primarily within the context of the eucharistic celebration.

Likewise, in I Corinthians 11, Paul's rebuke to the community provides us with a distinct picture of what the eucharist was to mean for the early Christians:

> But in the following instructions I do not commend you, because when you come together it is not for the better but for the worse. When you meet together, it is not the Lord's supper that you eat. For in eating, each one goes ahead with his own meal, and one is hungry and another drunk . . . Whoever, therefore, eats the bread or drinks the cup of the Lord in an unworthy manner will be guilty of profaning the body and blood of the Lord. For any one who eats and drinks without discerning the body eats and drinks judgement upon himself. (I Corinthians 11: 17, 20-21,27,29, RSV)

Paul's concern in this letter is obvious: some members of the community were eating the agape meal without taking into account the meaning behind the celebration of the eucharist which was to follow. Sharing and equality between members of the community were becoming obscured. Without this essential element, however, there could be no genuine celebration of the eucharist.

Moreover, for Paul and the early Church, the celebration of the eucharist was the place where Christians joined together not only to eat the body of Christ, but, more importantly, to *become* the body of Christ. During this time, the real presence of Christ was understood in a much broader sense than it was in the centuries that followed. Rather than isolating the presence of Christ in the elements of bread and wine alone, the early Church recognized Christ's fuller presence in the Christian community. Paul's letter to the Corinthians illuminates this point:

> When [Paul] speaks of "discerning the body," he is not referring primarily to a recognition of the real presence of Christ in the eucharistic species but rather to the recognition of Christ in the organic unity that exists . . . To discern the body is to grasp the indissoluble link between the eucharistic action and the community that is created and sustained by that action.[78]

For the early Christians, then, the building up of a genuine community based on sharing and service was indicative of the real presence of Christ in the eucharist.

For the first few centuries of Christendom, this social, communitarian perception of the eucharist continued to have precedence over the view of the eucharist as the elements of bread and wine. St. John Chrysostom, in 400 A.D., clearly showed this precedence with the following exhortation: "Do you want to honor Christ's body? Then do not honor him here in the church with silken garments while neglecting him outside where he is cold and naked . . . First fill him when he is hungry; then use the means you have left to adorn his table."[79] For the early Christians, then, the eucharist was a social act that explicitly demanded service of others in order for it to be authentically celebrated. It was not to be an end unto itself, but an action which led to service and giving of self.

Eucharist from the Fourth to the Twentieth Century

According to many liberation theologians, it was after these first few centuries of Christianity that the meaning which was given to the eucharist by Jesus at the Last Supper and retained by the early Church began to be distorted. For one thing, the communitarian aspect of the eucharist which was so important to Paul began to be subordinated to the objective real presence of Christ under the species of bread and wine. The actions of sharing and service carried out by the eucharistic community were no longer seen as the most important proclamation of Christ's presence. Thus,

> . . . the presence of Christ "placed" by the Bible primarily in the community . . . became primarily a thing generated as the result of a cosmological concept of the presence of Christ, which involved the accompanying dangers of misrepresentation, of magic, and of ritualism, and consequently of dehistoricalization.[80]

In addition, the emphasis on uniformity and ritual in the Mass, the notion that the eucharist could be a means with which to bless people who rarely received, and the fact that attendance at Mass had become an obligation worthy of merit, all tended to make the eucharist an individualistic, other-worldly ritual which had no relation to the everyday lives of those who attended.[81]   Most significant for many liberation theologians is the fact that the eucharist had often gone hand in hand with large scale exploitation, be it during the period of colonization or later, when the rich countries exploited the poor. Far from contesting the widespread desecration of countries and native peoples, the celebration of the eucharist seemed to legitimize (or at least justify) the exploitation insofar as it allowed and even encouraged exploiter and exploited to sit at the same table. This recognition has led many to the conclusion that the eucharist itself is in captivity and is therefore in need of liberation from world power and the status quo.[82]

Starting with the liturgical movement of the twentieth century, there came a gradual recognition that something was missing in the celebration of the eucharist and that the situation had to be rectified. In the 1960's, as we have seen, the *Constitution on the Sacred Liturgy* of Vatican II initiated many helpful changes: active participation was promoted and, to a large degree, rigidity in ceremony and ritual was eased. Despite specific changes, however, the essential meaning of the eucharist has still not been completely restored. Unfortunately, the changes which were made were of an external nature (songs, language, ritual) and had little to do with the social aspect of the eucharist: ". . . all these changes are marginal to the main problem that the whole Mass is still a bulwark of social conservatism and not yet a means of human liberation."[83]

3. Rediscovering the Link Between the Eucharist, Justice and Liberation

Liberation theologians now insist that, if the meaning of the eucharist is to be restored, the essential link between the eucharist and justice found in the biblical and early Christian accounts of the eucharist must be reestablished. Put plainly: ". . . the eucharist cannot be celebrated in the spirit of Jesus when that celebration is unaccompanied by a hunger and thirst for justice."[84]   The missing link between the celebration of the eucharist on Sunday and working for justice the other six days of the week must be recovered and emphasized.

This is not to say, of course, that doctrinal issues and debates over the real presence and the sacrifice of the Mass are unimportant. They are, however, facets of the eucharist which have been over-emphasized throughout the centuries to the detriment of another, equally important aspect: the relationship between the celebration of the eucharist and justice for the world:

> In so far as this liberating action for justice is absent from the Mass, to this extent we have to say an essential element of the eucharistic mystery is missing. This thesis that Christian action for justice is bound up with the celebration of the eucharist is as important as the other basic doctrines of the eucharist such as the real presence, the sacrifice of Calvary, the paschal meal, and the memorial.[85]

It is this link, therefore, that liberation theologians are seeking to recover.

As a result of searching for the biblical and early Christian meaning of the eucharist and re-discovering the necessary link that must exist between worship and justice, liberation theologians have concluded that the eucharist *must* be connected with human liberation. "The Eucharist," Balasuriya declares, "has to be related positively to human liberation if it is to be faithful to its origins and its performance."[86] The eucharist must therefore be a memorial, a celebration and an application of the meaning of Jesus' life and death of service and self-giving for others.

In order for the eucharist to be related to human liberation, participants must be alerted to the fundamental meaning of that in which they are participating. "An essential element in the celebration of the eucharist should be raising the consciousness of those who worship to their responsibility for effecting a liberating change in the world around us and the creation of a more just society in the service of the kingdom of God."[87] In order for those who participate in the eucharistic celebration to be true to its meaning, they must be made aware of the implication of that celebration for their own lives.

If not, the entire meaning of the eucharist as a means of human liberation will be falsified.

A meaningful celebration of the eucharist *must* therefore raise certain questions about the authenticity of what is being celebrated. However, liberation theologians are swift to make a distinction at this point. Leonardo Boff puts it in these terms: "By no means am I calling into question the theological context of the sacrament, with its effect *ex opere operato* and the real presence of Christ. What I am questioning is the use we make of the eucharistic celebration on these occasions."[88] Thus, the concern on the part of the liberation theologians is not so much with the theology of the eucharist as with the authenticity of the celebration. It *must* be a consciousness-raising event in order to be true to its meaning.

For some, this means demanding the exclusion of certain people from the celebration or even suspending the celebration. These people have a valid concern. Is a Mass celebrated with those responsible for the torture and death of civilians in fact true to its meaning of a celebration of community? Aldo Vannucchi questions: "Is there room for the oppressors and the oppressed at the Lord's Supper to partake of the Eucharist? . . . What must be done in order that liberation is evidenced precisely at the time of the Eucharist? Should the celebration be suspended in certain times and situations?"[89]

Others are insisting on the need for occasional "protest Masses" such as those that are being celebrated in some parts of Latin America. According to proponents, the Mass should, on certain occasions, serve as consciousness-raising events which protest against the injustices and oppression of humanity: ". . . l'eucharistie doit être un puissant cri d'alarme et de protestation, quelque chose qui vient troublé les consciences et éveiller des résponsabilités politico-sociales."[90] For people such as Segundo Galilea, any celebration which is true to the meaning of the eucharist cannot help but be a protest against oppression. By proclaiming the sole lordship of Christ, the eucharist is excluding any system which claims to have Lordship over a people: "à la messe, on proclame non seulement que le Christ est l'unique Seigneur, mais encore que sa seigneurie exclut tout autre seigneurie sur les hommes."[91]

The problem that such a celebration could cause for any oppressive regime is obvious: the liturgy would become a subversive activity with political consequences that could ultimately destroy an oppressive system. Just how far most eucharistic celebrations are from this ideal, however, is most clearly exemplified by Joseph Gelineau:

> . . . totalitarian political regimes which react adversely to the Church begin by forbidding Christians any form of self-organized action in society; they then prohibit or supervise religious instruction and preaching; but in general they allow worship as inoffensive. Moreover they sometimes consider the liturgy to be useful because it inculcates respect for the ruling order and submission to the established powers whatever they may be.[92]

The implication of this statement is profoundly disturbing: the celebration of the eucharist is not living up to its full potential as a liberating factor in society.

Regardless of how effective or ineffective most eucharistic celebrations are at bringing out this aspect of the eucharist, such a discussion nonetheless raises the issue of the place of politics in worship. As with most matters, there are two extremes to this issue: those who demand that politics be kept out of liturgy entirely and those who perceive the eucharist to be a forum for promoting specific causes and concerns. Neither extreme is true to the authentic nature of the eucharist.[93] Rather, the truth lies somewhere in the middle. Most theologians do insist that eucharistic celebrations, by their very character, are necessarily political events. If, as Herman Schmidt indicates, "politics is a human activity . . . Politics is necessary in all situations experienced by [humanity] . . . The idea of politics is not restricted, therefore, to the state with its political parties."[94] Then the eucharistic celebration as a gathering of particular people at a particular time and place is in fact a political reality. The celebration of the eucharist cannot take place outside of this reality and this historical situation, but must be a part of it with all that that entails. To evade the political aspect of the eucharistic celebration is either to give implicit assent to injustice and oppression or else to become otherworldly: "to attempt an ostensibly apolitical liturgy in a world essentially political is absurd—unless one wants to banish the Eucharist from history."[95]

There are obvious dangers which are inherent in such an approach to the eucharist. The greatest, of course, is the risk that considerations of faith will be subordinated to those of society and politics, with too little attention being paid to the faith aspect of the celebration.[96] The celebration of the eucharist in this case would come to be seen merely as a political weapon or statement. This is undoubtedly a very real danger. Despite this danger, however, most liberation theologians insist that the eucharistic celebration must be political to some extent if it is to be true to its function and meaning of liberation. Moreover, it is not a danger only for liberation theology. All theology runs the risk of being used to sanction a certain political system. A classic example of this is the Dutch Reformed Church's stance on apartheid.

If it is an authentic celebration, the eucharist should never be understood simply as an exhibition at which the people are spectators. In accord with Vatican II, Aldo Vannucchi insists that ". . . the eucharist is not a spectacle to be seen or endured, but action . . . that involves us in the same process, breaking the bread as [Jesus] broke it, washing the feet of others as he did . . ."[97] In order to be true to its inner meaning, the eucharistic celebration must move from thought to action. To be celebrated in the Spirit of Jesus, the eucharist must move people to work towards the building of a just world order. To receive Christ in the eucharist is to be transformed to do what he did: live for others. "In worship and in the eucharist [people] are taken up into this eschatological process of the setting free of the world to be a kingdom of glory."[98] Properly celebrated, the eucharist should effect a transformation in lifestyle which would commit people to work for the realization of the Kingdom of God. "A community celebration of the eucharist solemnly commits all Christians to struggle actively against everything that discriminates against and disintegrates humanity."[99] To celebrate the eucharist, therefore, is to take the pledge to work for that of which the eucharist is a foretaste.

A word of caution is necessary at this point: the Kingdom of God can never be identified with a particular political system that is brought about by humans in history. The work of justice that will bring about the Kingdom is God's alone. "[Humanity's] politics does not make the kingdom of God, but He makes His kingdom come by means of those who welcome his justice and love."[100] God works through people to establish the Kingdom. Those who are participants in the eucharist can only work towards the establishment of a just world. In the end, the achievement is God's.

In today's world, the physical act of sharing goods is one tangible way of working towards the realization of the Kingdom. According to liberation theologians, this action should be the outcome of an authentic celebration of the eucharist. The sharing of bread and wine at the eucharist should lay the foundations for how all material things should be used:

> . . . built into the Eucharist, therefore, is a demand for the just distribution of the world's wealth. To share the eucharistic bread is to say, using symbols, that this is how [people] should be using all material things; this places sharing at the basis of Christianity.[101]

The celebration of the eucharist presents us with the challenge to radically commit ourselves to the building of a just world order. To receive the token of sharing in the eucharist is a commission for us to do likewise: "Since food is shared around this table, it is also to be shared around other tables."[102]

In order to get a more basic understanding of what sharing is, people need to get in touch with the fundamental experience of hunger. "Hunger is a total, global experience."[103] Those who are hungry are not only those who are starving for physical sustenance, but also those who are famished for love and human fulfillment. One type of hunger is on the physical level, while the other is on the emotional or spiritual level. Despite this difference, however, the two levels are complementary and interdependent.

> It has been observed in the contemporary world that those who most insistently complain as adults of finding that hunger [for human fulfillment] unfulfilled, are also those who individually or collectively are amassing and hoarding and wasting so much of the material resources of the world, that others are kept on the verge of starvation in great numbers.[104]

As a result, all people—both oppressors and oppressed—need to be liberated from these oppressive situations.

At first glance, it may seem like such an explanation in some way justifies those who hoard goods for themselves. This is simply not true. The point is that physical hunger ". . . is not due to overpopulation but to patterns of land and food distribution."[105] When looked at in the light of the two different levels of hunger, then it becomes evident that the suffering of hunger is due to warped human behavior which is intent only on self-preservation. Only by correcting this attitude and replacing it with one of sharing will physical hunger cease to be the overwhelming problem that it is today.

The logical outcome of a meaningful eucharistic celebration should be this type of sharing. In fact, some theologians are even going so far as to say that this aspect of sharing is the very *essence* of the eucharist. Mark Searle, for example, proposes that:

> . . . it used to be thought that the "matter" of the sacraments was bread, wine, oil, water and so forth. More recently there has been a healthy tendency to suggest that it is not the bread that constitutes the sacramental sign of the eucharist . . . but bread that is broken and shared, the cup of wine passed around for all to drink . . . .[106]

Accordingly, it is in the action of sharing that Christ's presence is affirmed.

4. The Eucharistic Community as the Body of Christ

When all is said and done, however, the most important dimension of the eucharist lies in its ability to form a community which is committed to the work of justice and liberation. "Hence our pre-occupation has not to be so much with the eucharistic service for its own sake, but, rather, with the building of a real sharing community that is concerned with the whole society."[107] The eucharist cannot remain an end unto itself, but must be related to what is occurring in the world. Only then can it retain its power to transform.

It is, furthermore, within the context of a eucharistic community that one experiences the real presence of Christ at its most profound level. I Corinthians 11 is cited as ample evidence that ". . . it is not just bread alone which is being called the body of Christ but the community of people drawn and assembled together as a new reality in sharing the eucharistic species."[108] It is apparent from Paul's letter that that which invalidated the eucharist for the early Christians was not the lack of correct rites, but rather, the lack of a proper eucharistic community. The building of a true community must become *the* major issue in contemporary eucharistic theology and must be given precedence over matters of doctrine or ritual.

A celebration of the eucharist which keeps the image of the larger body of Christ foremost in mind retains its power to transform society. This is not meant to imply, of course, that the distinctive real presence of Christ in the bread and wine is unimportant. To the contrary, it is Christ's presence in the bread and wine which provides the *basis* for the formation of the larger body of Christ. The eucharistic community is transformed into the larger body of Christ because it is *really* Christ who, in the sharing of the bread and wine, calls us to be united and to transform society.[109] Liberation theology's emphasis, therefore, is not so much on the fact of Christ's presence in the bread and wine as it is on the *purpose* behind that presence: to unite and transform the participants and thereby enable them to create a new societal reality of sharing and service.

Inner conversion is an important outcome of an authentic eucharistic celebration. Without it, the larger body of Christ which is based on sharing and service, would not become a reality.

> . . . the Eucharistic signs and symbols do not of themselves change social, political and economic structures; but they should change 700 million hearts and minds, grace them to admit the oppressions of which they are victims and for which they are responsible, inspire them to work with others for the coming of a kingdom characterized by justice and love.[110]

Ideally, personal transformation should result in a corresponding transformation of society. Together, the Christian community can be true to the liberative message of the eucharist. Together, individuals can take action against those injustices which are contrary to the true meaning of the eucharist:

> The Eucharist elicits the expectation that the church will be actively involved in the transformation of the human community. The family that eats together is expected to stay together, sharing and ministering one to the other in order to eliminate the effects of poverty, suffering and oppression.[111]

Transformation of society, then, consists of service towards and sharing with others. The eucharist and the community which celebrates it should be an impetus for this metamorphosis.

One problem that arises, however, is that any eucharistic community which could have this effect on society must be a group of people who know each other on an intimate basis rather than a large, impersonal parish. Effective action can best be carried out by a community whose members know and care for each other in a significant manner. This ". . . means that a parish of one thousand or five thousand or ten thousand persons cannot easily become a relevant group for a meaningful and truthful eucharistic celebration."[112] To truly learn and live out the inner meaning of the eucharist, the celebrating community must of necessity be comprised of a small number of members.

It is these small base communities which are in large part responsible for the ever increasing demand to understand the inner meaning of the eucharist: ". . . today the main trends in the evolution of the eucharistic theology and devotion take place outside the official circles concerned with the control of the Eucharist, i.e. the Roman curia and the local diocesan authorities."[113] This is not to say that the official Church is completely denying or ignoring the necessary link between the eucharist and liberation. The 42nd International Eucharistic Congress in 1981, for example, which had as its theme "Eucharistic Bread Broken for a New World," sought to establish the link between the shared meal of the eucharist and the responsibility of the eucharistic community to take action to relieve world hunger. At the Congress, it was officially concluded that a "synthesis between the eucharistic faith and efforts to satisfy human hunger is essential if the symbolic reality of the Eucharist is to remain alive and authentic."[114]

Despite such sanctioning from the official Church, however, theologians such as Tissa Balasuriya are insisting that most eucharistic reforms which are ratified by the official Church are totally inadequate for dealing with the concrete situation of oppression.[115] As a result, the renewal of the eucharist is taking place apart from the official Church. Edward Schillebeeckx, however, contends that *any* renewal within the Church usually begins as an illegal deviation. Renewal, therefore, usually begins with the people, rather than being imposed on them from above.[116] Genuine renewal of the eucharist, then, will most likely arise from out of the small base communities.

Arising inevitably from the effort to recover the inner meaning of the eucharist is the issue of the nature of the priesthood and the need for an ordained priest as presider at the celebrations. The starting point for such a consideration is the undeniable right of a community to be able to celebrate the eucharist. The final document from Puebla, for example, follows the teachings of Vatican II by insisting that "the Eucharist is the root and pivot of the whole community."[117] The problem, however, is that eucharistic celebrations are often impossible since many base communities do not have an ordained priest living in their midst. The shortage of priests, therefore, leads to a decline in the celebration of the eucharist.

This shortage of priests, according to Balasuriya, is not only due to the obligatory celibacy that is forced upon priests, although this has led to a marked decrease in the priesthood. Just as important, however, is the fact that more and more priests are beginning to recognize the irrelevance of the celebration of the eucharist over which they preside. And, "when he begins to lose faith in its actual impact he begins to question the meaning of his whole life."[118] If the eucharist is properly understood, but is not being practised in a like manner, the celebrant will call into question his whole vocation which is centered around the eucharist. A change in the conception of the eucharist will therefore lead to a change in the nature of the priesthood.

The problem of infrequent eucharistic celebrations in the last few years has led to the re-examination of the presiders of the eucharist. Phillip Berryman, for example, rightly indicates that "if a 'priest shortage' makes [the celebration of the Eucharist] impossible, the Catholic system for preparing and ordaining priests should be questioned and re-examined."[119] By studying the historical development of this system, theologians have discovered that it was not until the second millennium that the present system of ordination came into being. In the first millennium, office bearers were to be called, appointed and accepted by a specific community. These leaders, chosen by the community, were also those who presided over the eucharist: "Whoever was competent to lead the community was also *ipso facto* the leader in the Eucharist."[120] The most important factor involved was being chosen by the community. By the second millennium, however, the eucharist had become clericalized and could only be celebrated by a validly ordained priest. The celebration was regarded not so much as an action of the people in which all took part, but rather, as an action of God through the intermediary of the priest.[121] In addition, the priest no longer had to be called and accepted by the community but was appointed by the bishop; the local community no longer had any significant input into who would become their leader.

After taking into account the historical system of ordination, many theologians are now advocating alternative forms of leadership: "In principle, the local community should satisfy its own ministerial needs by having ministers from among its members."[122] The presider at the eucharist should be a community leader. However, since enforced celibacy is a requirement and few members of a community are likely to be celibate, this is usually not an option. According to Leonardo Boff, this cannot be an excuse:

> . . . to deprive thousands upon thousands of communities of the sacrament of the Eucharist, and of the incomparable benefits of having an ordained minister, through inflexibility in maintaining a tradition that has bound a necessary service (that of priesthood) to a free charism (that of celibacy) is tantamount to an unlawful violation of the rights of the faithful.[123]

One possible response, then, is to change the requirements for ordination: ordain married people and make celibacy an optional part of ordination. It appears unlikely, however, that this solution will be accepted by the Roman authorities in the near future.

Another solution to this crisis would be to allow the non-ordained community co-ordinator or leader, acting as extra-ordinary minister, to consecrate the eucharist. By virtue of the faith of the community in Christ's presence in the celebration, and based on the priesthood of all believers, the eucharist would be valid, though not sacramentally full:

> The absence of an ordained minister, in the presence of a need and desire for the Eucharist, does not seem to constitute an absolute obstacle to the eucharistic celebration. The common priesthood of all the faithful would permit the president of the community to render visible—sacramental—the priestly, eucharistic action of Christ.[124]

Indeed, more and more Roman Catholics in Latin America (and even in many other parts of the world) are joining together under the leadership of the community co-ordinator for a special celebration. Boff describes this celebration as follows:

> This community celebration ought not to be called the mass, since the mass is a rigorously defined reality, theologically, liturgically, and canonically. It could be called the celebration of the Lord's Supper, however, as it would have a ritual organized by the community itself, in which would clearly appear the memorial character of meal, sacrifice and eucharistic presence of Christ.[125]

The celebration of the Lord's Supper, while not the Mass, greatly resembles the eucharistic liturgy. It is a mixture of scriptural readings, shared reflections, acts of repentance and conversion, offerings of either the region's produce or of bread and wine, a reading of the account of the Last Supper, the Lord's Prayer, communion and a commitment of service.[126] It is, therefore, a celebration which closely resembles the eucharistic celebrations of the early Christians.

While the official Church may not find this alternative totally acceptable, it is one which nevertheless needs to be acknowledged. Without trying to dispense with the traditional mass formula, the celebration of the Lord's Supper as described above is one community's attempt to follow Jesus' command to "Do this in memory of me" in spite of the lack of an ordained priest. Thus, as many liberation theologians are concluding: "Perhaps the church ought to envision different ways of celebrating the Lord's Supper, ranging from Mass with the people of God, the traditional formula and still practically the only one in use today, to the 'breaking of the bread' as it was celebrated in the early Christian communities."[127]

Conclusion: Vatican Response to Liberation Theology

In many ways, the re-interpretation of the eucharist as advocated by liberation theologians differs greatly from the standard understanding of the eucharist. Moving away from the emphasis on the real presence of Christ in the bread and wine, liberation theologians are insisting that Christ's real presence be recognized in a wider context: a community of sharing and service that comes into being as a result of the authentic celebration of the eucharist. The eucharist, these theologians maintain, must be integrally related to human liberation and justice. Those who have celebrated Jesus' giving of self for others must be transformed and take that liberative message into the world by following Jesus' example. The eucharist cannot remain an end to itself, but must be the impetus for working towards justice and liberation.

Such an understanding, however, has wide-reaching effects. Not only is traditional eucharistic doctrine subordinated to the new emphasis on service, sharing and community, such an understanding also calls into question the meaningfulness of the standard celebration of the eucharist, of the eucharistic community and of the priesthood. Is it any wonder that the official Church finds some difficulties with such a re-interpretation?

Be this as it may, very little has been said by the Vatican on this reinterpretation of the eucharist except within the context of liberation theology in general. With regards to liberation theology in general, however, much has been said and done. The Vatican has, for example, taken action against a number of liberation theologians: "Theologian Gustavo Gutierrez of Peru was under unceasing attack for three years, and Brazilian Leonardo Boff faced similar onslaughts."[128] Priests, too, have been pressured to stay out of politics and those in government have been forced to resign. As well, the 1984 *Instruction on Certain Aspects of the "Theology of Liberation"* by the Vatican Congregation for the Doctrine of the Faith outlined in detail the problems that it found with liberation theology. All of this combined gives, according to Berryman, "strong indications that this was indeed a systematic attack by the Vatican aimed at delegitimizing liberation theology in all its forms."[129]

In all fairness, we must acknowledge the fact that not all of the response from the Vatican has been negative. The *Instruction*, for example, begins by outlining what it deems to be the positive aspects of liberation theology. The follow-up document in 1986—*Instruction on Christian Freedom and Liberation*—while still critical, was more positive than the former document. In fact, the positive outweighs the negative in this document to such an extent that Robert McAfee Brown claims that "it gives a clear signal that the Vatican has decided not to throw down the gauntlet to liberation theologians."[130]

While recognizing certain positive aspects of liberation theology, however, the 1984 *Instruction* is most definitely critical of certain tenets.[131] One major criticism found in the document is the assertion that liberation theology is reductionist; that is, that it places politics before religion, and material conditions before spiritual concerns. At one point, for example, the *Instruction* claims that faith and the Gospel are reduced to some earthly ideology and thus, that the core of salvation is the struggle for justice: "To some it even seems that the necessary struggle for human justice and freedom in the economic and political sense constitutes the whole essence of salvation.

For them, the Gospel is reduced to a purely earthly gospel."[132]

In another place, the *Instruction* warns against reducing sin to social structures and thereby making liberation from temporal, earthly servitude more important than liberation from sin: "Nor can one localize evil principally or uniquely in bad social, political or economic "structures" as though all other evils came from them so that the creation of the "new man" would depend on the establishment of different economic and sociopolitical structures."[133] Liberation theology is also accused of a reductionist reading of the Bible. By re-reading Scripture "politically," the *Instruction* claims, liberation theology tends to make the political aspect of the reading the only component.

The *Instruction* also criticizes liberation theology on the grounds that it leads to the undermining of church authority. By emphasizing the need for a church of the people (which is ultimately a church of the class, according to the document), liberation theologians are supposedly denouncing church authority as classist:

> Building on such a conception of the church of the people, a critique of the very structures of the church is developed . . . is a denunciation of members of the hierarchy and the magisterium as objective representatives of the ruling class which has to be opposed.[134]

Those who do not share the same attitudes as liberation theologians are those who, according to the document, are denounced as belonging to the oppressors. As a result, the Church itself is divided and church authority is undermined.

The major criticism in the *Instruction* is of liberation theology's use of Marxism. The purpose of the document, it is stated, is

> . . . to draw the attention of pastors, theologians and all the faithful to the deviations and risks of deviations, damaging to the faith and to Christian living, that are brought about by certain forms of liberation theology which use, in an insufficiently critical manner, concepts borrowed from various currents of Marxist thoughts.[135]

A total, unqualified acceptance of Marxism in the first place tends to legitimize the use of violence in all forms: "to the violence which constitutes the relationship of the domination of the rich over the poor, there corresponds the counterviolence of the revolution, by means of which this domination will be reversed."[136]

More importantly, according to the *Instruction*, because of their acceptance of Marxism, liberation theologians tend to make the class struggle a necessity for Christians. Thus, "they pervert the Christian meaning of the poor, and they transform the fight for the rights of the poor into a class struggle."[137] As a result, everything—faith and theology included—becomes subordinated to the struggle.

It is within this context that the document makes explicit reference to the perception of the eucharist within the context of liberation theology. As a result of the influence of Marxism, the *Instruction* claims, the eucharist is being used as a tool for the class struggle. By questioning whether or not Christians who belong to different social classes can share in the same eucharist and still retain its authentic meaning, liberation theologians are, according to the *Instruction*, distorting the meaning of the eucharist. Thus, "the eucharist is no longer to be understood as the real sacramental presence of the reconciling sacrifice and as the gift of the body and blood of Christ. It becomes the celebration of the people in their struggle."[138]

The most objectionable consequence of this type of eucharistic celebration which epitomizes the class struggle is that it destroys the unity of the Church:

> Unity, reconciliation and communion in love are no longer seen as a gift we receive from Christ. It is the historical class of the poor who by means of their struggle will build unity. For them, the struggle of the classes is the way to unity . . . the unity of the church is radically denied.[139]

The unity of the Church in the celebration of the eucharist is a primary concern in the *Instruction*.

At this point, the question must be raised: should the authentic celebration of the eucharist be denied in order that uniformity of celebration be maintained? Is the so-called unity of the Church more important than justice? To this, the liberation theologians would answer with a resounding "NO!" It is an answer which the official Church should not try to ignore. Uniformity and unity cannot be thought of as synonymous terms. One cannot and should not, in the name of uniformity, force P.W. Botha and Desmond Tutu to partake of the same eucharist and still pretend that it is an authentic celebration for them both.

Moreover, although the official Church disagrees (on the grounds that it destroys Church unity) with those liberation theologians who wish to exclude certain people (e.g. oppressors) from the eucharistic celebrations, this same Church does not hesitate to bar divorced Catholics from publicly receiving the eucharist. Boff makes much of this point, stating that "the Church would not be judging the subjective culpability of the oppressor or agent, any more than it judges the subjective culpability of the divorced person whom it forbids to receive the eucharist in public."[140] To most liberation theologians, therefore, it is clear that impartiality is not an option: either communities must stop celebrating the eucharist or else take its implications seriously, even if this means barring those who are oppressors from its celebration.[141]

The logical conclusion would be the acceptance on the part of the official Church of different ways of celebrating the eucharist. While the different celebrations such as those experienced by the basic Christian communities may at present be regarded as deviations from the norm, they are obviously fulfilling a great need in those places where they are being celebrated. If the traditional means of participating in the eucharist are totally inadequate and irrelevant for so many people (to the extent that they are no longer attending Mass) a new means of partaking of the eucharist which draws people to its celebration can only be a positive factor for the Christian community. Such celebrations are a force to be reckoned with. Regardless of the official Church's stance at present, the grassroots communities which celebrate the eucharist in this way are going to continue to do so. Persecution and isolation by the official Church will not cause the movement to die, but perhaps even to flourish. The official Church will either have to accept and welcome their position, create a viable alternative or, if worse comes to worse, watch the Church become split in two.

Discussion Questions

1. What is liberation theology? How is it done?
2. Why is a social dimension necessary to Christian faith in general and the renewal of the eucharist in particular?
3. Briefly describe a basic Christian community.
4. How and why, according to liberation theology, has the traditional perception of the sacraments been distorted?
5. Segundo claims that the crisis which is occurring in sacramental theology is essentially a crisis in community? Explain. Do you agree?
6. When read from within the context of liberation theology, what do the New Testament accounts of the institution of the eucharist and the washing of the feet tell us about the meaning of the eucharist?
7. What elements have led to the distortion of the meaning of the eucharist over the centuries?
8. According to many liberation theologians, the essential link between the eucharist, liberation and justice must be re-discovered and re-emphasized. What are some steps they suggest must be taken towards this?
9. What role do you think politics play in the celebration of the eucharist? Explain your answer.
10. On what grounds do liberation theologians base their demand for the re-evaluation of the requirements demanded of the presider of the eucharist?
11. In your opinion, is the celebration of the Lord's Supper in the base communities as described by Boff an authentic celebration of the eucharist? Why or why not?
12. What aspects of the reinterpretation of the eucharist within the context of liberation theology does Rome find unacceptable? Do you agree? Why or why not?
13. What dimensions of liberation theology's reinterpretation of the eucharist do you find most helpful to your own personal understanding of the eucharist? Explain.

Chapter Five

The Future of the Eucharist

AS THE CENTRAL FOCUS OF OUR LIVES AS ROMAN CATHOLICS, is it any wonder that literally *centuries* have been spent developing and formulating the proper understanding of the eucharist? It is *the* foremost situation in which our faith as Catholics is expressed. Sadly enough, however, the centrality of the eucharist is at risk. Obstacles which are both theological and pastoral in nature are threatening to push the eucharist into a subsidiary position for an ever increasing number of Roman Catholics. Eucharistic doctrine, because of the medieval terms in which it is couched, is unintelligible and irrelevant to a large percentage of Catholics. As a result, those who attend the eucharistic celebration often do so with little understanding of the true meaning behind the eucharist. For many people, moreover, the Sunday celebration appears to have little connection to what is happening the other six days of the week. Low attendance at the Sunday liturgy gives witness to the fact that these Catholics are either no longer attending the liturgy or are searching out smaller, more autonomous gatherings. Even more frustrating is the reality that those who *do* wish to participate in the Sunday eucharistic liturgy are now being thwarted. The ever-growing shortage of ordained priests means that more and more Catholics are forced to live without a weekly (or in some cases, even monthly) eucharistic celebration.

Happily, the direction which eucharistic theology has been taking in the years since the Second Vatican Council is a reason for hope. More and more theologians are recognizing the potential of the celebration of the eucharist. If properly understood and authentically celebrated, the eucharist has the capacity to transform not only individual lives, but all of human history. Unfortunately, if the eucharist were to remain meaningless and irrelevant for the majority of Roman Catholics, this transforming power would be lost. In recognition of this fact, theologians such as Schillebeeckx, Balasuriya and Boff are striving, each in their own way, to make the eucharist more relevant to the ordinary Catholic layperson. They seek to liberate the eucharist from any traditional trappings which may inhibit people from fully understanding its true meaning and fulfilling its true potential.

Fundamental to these new developments which are occurring in eucharistic theology is the renewed appreciation of the various dimensions of the eucharist. Indeed, it is becoming increasingly apparent that no *one* attempt at explaining the eucharist can ever be fully encompassing. Doctrinal definitions such as those developed during the Middle Ages, while basic to a proper appreciation of the eucharist, can never fully capture its multi-faceted essence. Recognition that the eucharist is multi-dimensional means that emphasis is being transferred from doctrinal issues of sacrifice and real presence to other equally important dimensions. This is not to deny or belittle the eucharistic doctrine which has been formulated and handed on through the centuries. These basic ideas are in fact being renewed and given new meaning by modern insights: "The old elements are there, but they are now part of a new synthesis."[1] However, in light of the fact that doctrinal matters have dominated eucharistic theology for centuries, many contemporary theologians are now exploring other, previously unemphasized facets of the eucharist.

Theologians such as Schillebeeckx and certain liberation theologians who have dealt with the eucharist strive to build on the existing deposit of eucharistic theology, using it to seek out answers to the problems which are now facing the eucharist.[2] In response to problems such as the unintelligibility of doctrine or the seeming irrelevance of the eucharist celebration for many Catholics, these theologians are shifting their attention away from a highly Scholastic insistence on the objective, doctrinal elements of the eucharist to the more subjective aspect of the *people* who are celebrating the eucharist. Schillebeeckx' shift from an Aristotelian framework to one of interpersonal relationships means that the emphasis is placed on the existential experience of the person who is celebrating the eucharist. His concern, while still doctrinal, focuses not solely on the doctrine, but on what meaning and significance it has for people—the deepening of the personal relationship with Christ. Liberation theologians expand this notion by focusing their attention on the *effect* that the eucharistic celebration will have on those who participate in it. Doctrine is retained, but transformation of life and action become the primary concern.

For both, the *fact* of the real presence, well established during the Middle Ages, is given less emphasis than the *purpose* of the real presence—the deepening of the intimate relationship with Christ which transforms individuals and empowers them to transform the world. Hence, those gathered to celebrate the eucharist are being given priority over the elements of bread and wine.

Common Ground

The approaches to eucharistic theology which have developed over the last thirty years are indeed diverse. They have arisen from different cultural and geographical backgrounds, for different reasons, at different times in history and in response to different situations. Be this as it may, however, there exists between them certain significant areas of common ground which seem to point the way to the future of eucharistic theology.

1. Refusal to Separate Faith and Life

Eucharistic theology today is characterized by an adamant refusal to separate faith and life or, more specifically, life within the Sunday eucharistic liturgy and that which exists during the rest of the week. In previous centuries, the liturgy was often looked upon as an otherworldly flight from the problems of the world which had no relationship to daily living. The overemphasis on the sacredness of the liturgy meant that the liturgy had little rootedness in reality.[3]

In recent years, more and more people are staying away from the Sunday eucharistic celebration precisely because they see no relation between Sunday and the other six days of the week.[4] This is a fundamental and wide-sweeping problem. Contemporary theologians such as Boff, Schillebeeckx and Balasuriya insist that if the eucharistic liturgy is to be alive, dynamic and relevant, it *must* be related to all aspects of daily life. The liturgy cannot be an escape from reality, but rather a celebration of that reality. This is a sobering reminder that the Church and the liturgy do not exist apart from, but are an integral part *of* the world. Aldo Vannuchi sums up best: "True liturgy is wholly engrafted into the reality of the world."[5]

Much of this emphasis on the need to integrate the liturgy and life derives from the radical expansion of the concept of grace which presupposes the presence of grace in all aspects of human life and acknowledges the sacredness of human history. God is not divorced from human life, but rather already present in every aspect of life. Human life and history are, therefore, *the* place where God is revealed to humanity. Accordingly, humanity must be the focus of eucharistic theology. Schillebeeckx, for example, insists that, since the eucharist is intended for humans, it must be related to human experience. As a result, he develops his understanding of the eucharist around the framework of interpersonal relationships. Liberation theologians also ascertain that the eucharist must work from the basis of human experience. It must be a celebration of that which exists in daily life as well as a celebration which will effect a transformation in daily life:

> . . . any understanding of the Eucharist, if it is to be relevant and fruitful for the life of the Church in the

world today, must go beyond ritual concerns and beyond speculations about "presence," "meal or sacrifice," to face the very fundamental and concrete question of the quality of life in the eucharistic community and in the world.[6]

Coupled with this is the recognition that instead of stressing the sacredness of the eucharist, more emphasis must be placed on its integration with human life. As a result, the official Church is being urged to make all aspects of eucharistic theology concrete and grounded in history rather than abstract and otherworldly. In particular, the Church should strive to ground its eucharistic liturgies in the historical realities of the time and place in which they are celebrated. One simple example is to allow indigenous people to celebrate the eucharist with elements which are staples for them rather than insisting on the use of bread and wine. In the Philippines, for instance, wheat is not a staple good. As a result, "'bread is a luxury food of the middle and upper classes.' Rice would be more appropriate in this culture."[7] The Church should therefore be willing to move beyond the traditional understanding of the eucharist if it wishes to narrow the already existing chasm between life in the Church and life in the world.

2. The Eucharist as a Meal

Part of what is happening in contemporary eucharistic theology is a re-recognition that a meal is *the* basic structure of the eucharistic liturgy. Before the 1960's, the eucharist was thought of primarily in terms of the elements of bread and wine. In Vatican II and post-Vatican II theology, on the other hand, the eucharist is understood in a much broader context. The directives of the *Constitution on the Sacred Liturgy* which allowed communion under both species and communion with hosts consecrated at that liturgy helped to increase the sign value of the eucharist as a meal. To eat *and* drink of the newly consecrated bread and wine points clearly to the fact that the eucharistic celebration occurs within the context of a meal.

Moreover, contemporary theologians are insisting that it is the *total* complex of any human meal which actually makes up the eucharist. The eucharist consists not only of bread and wine, but of all factors which make up a meal: gathering, sharing stories and eating together. Furthermore, as a meal, the eucharist is not just food to look at, but food to share with one another. In this way, emphasis is shifted from the eucharist as an object of worship to the eucharist as a total action of worship.

Furthermore, renewed emphasis on the meal aspect of the eucharist also affects our understanding of the meaning behind the eucharist. Liberation theologians, for example, maintain that, as a meal, the eucharist must be a sign of sharing, forgiveness, unity and the abolition of injustice. This, in turn, presents a challenge to those who participate in its celebration. These very qualities of the meal must then be transferred to the daily lives of Christians. To forgive, share and be united in the eucharistic meal challenges us to forgive, share and be united in our daily meals.

3. The Importance of Community

Closely related to the perception of the eucharist as a meal is the renewed emphasis that is placed on the centrality of the community which gathers together for the eucharistic celebration. For many years, an excessive sense of individualism often characterized the celebration of the eucharist. Separate devotions such as reciting the Rosary during Mass seemed to imply that the eucharist was something between the individual and God. In recognition of this individualism, Vatican II places great emphasis on the fact that Christian worship is above all a public and communal experience. By acknowledging that Christ is truly present in all aspects of the liturgy, the *Constitution on the Sacred Liturgy* recognizes Christ's presence in the worshipping community as well as in its actions of prayer, song and response. Moreover, the *Constitution* indicates that the communal celebration of the sacraments is to be preferred over a private and individual ceremony: "Liturgical services are not private functions, but are celebrations of the

Church . . ."[8] Indeed, even the language which is used in the document expresses the importance of community. Rather than speaking in terms of "receiving" the eucharist, an expression which implies a personal and private act of one person, the *Constitution* uses the language of "celebration" which signifies a communal function in which everyone is involved. Communal celebration is therefore given priority over personal worship.

In addition, the desire to restore the essential meaning of the eucharist as it was celebrated in the first century has led many theologians to explore more deeply Paul's explanation of the eucharist in I Corinthians 11. As a result, attention is being focused on Christ's real presence in the gathered community rather than merely in the elements of bread and wine. It is in the community of believers that Christ's presence is most profoundly depicted. Schillebeeckx expresses it best when he writes:

> Like those early Christians, we too must experience this reality within the concrete context of our contemporary lives by constantly making present and reinterpreting here and now, by giving new life to, what these first Christians experienced in contact with the living Christ. The past is also a call to us now . . . to realize a fraternal community by participating in a Christian meal. The living Christ identifies himself with the community at table . . . [9]

Hence, the authentic celebration of the eucharist as a meal depends in large part on the community which is gathered.

Schillebeeckx, for instance, expands this renewed emphasis on community by maintaining that the presence of Christ in the eucharist cannot be understood apart from the larger presence of Christ in the community. Christ's presence in the elements has been broadened to include the larger realm of the community. In fact, for Schillebeeckx, the believing response of the community is a necessity for the complete realization of the real presence of Christ in the eucharist. The presence of Christ in the community is therefore central to Schillebeeckx' theology.

Despite his emphasis on the importance of the community, however, Schillebeeckx' central focus is nonetheless the real presence of Christ in the eucharist; the community is important, but it is still secondary. Liberation theologians such as Balasuriya and Boff, however, give the presence of Christ in the community precedence over his presence in the eucharist. They insist that it is in community that Christ's presence is most profound. Without the essential element of true community, there can be no genuine celebration of eucharist. It is the gathered community which enables Christ to be present among them. Without the wider presence of Christ in the community, Christ's presence in the bread and wine remains without significance. Thus, by focusing on the real presence of Christ in the community, the liberation theologians are emphasizing the reality of Christ's presence outside the elements of bread and wine to which it had previously been either limited (pre-Vatican II theology) or at least made secondary (Schillebeeckx' theology).[10]

4. Renewed Understanding of Church

The new direction in which eucharistic theology is moving is intricately linked with and has a profound influence on the new models of church which are emerging in Roman Catholicism. Previous to Vatican II, the Roman Catholic conception of church was highly institutional and exclusivistic. The Church was equated with the hierarchy. Members were those who adhered to certain doctrines, partook of the sacraments and obeyed the prescribed authorities. With the advent of Vatican II and the conception of the church as the pilgrim people of God, much of this was changed. Theologians began to recognize that no *one* model of the Church was sufficient. Rather, the church can best be understood by a number of different models.[11]

One such model which was introduced at Vatican II and expanded upon by theologians such as Schillebeeckx and Rahner is that of the church as the sacrament of Christ. According to this model, the church must make visible God's offer of himself through Christ to humanity. As a sign of the on-going presence of the risen Christ, the church must make God's love for humanity concrete and tangible through both worship and deed. There are, however, some limitations to the model of church as sacrament. Most notable, according to Richard McBrien, is the fact that such an understanding of the church remains too narrow: "[it] accords insufficient place for *diakonia* (service in the Church's mission to the world.)"[12] Nonetheless, while there is some validity to this criticism, this aspect of service is, at least to some extent, implicitly acknowledged in the image of church as sacrament. According to this understanding, the church is the basic sacrament insofar as it makes salvation available in a *tangible* and *historical* way. In using these words, the notion of service is, although not expressed in so many words, at least inferred.

Others have carried this element of service to a far greater and more explicit extent in their understanding of church. Liberation theologians insist that if the church is to be the sacrament of Christ, it must be a church of service to the poor. It must become a church which is characterized by concern for and service to others. The importance of the church lies not so much in its capacity to be the custodian of the faith as in its call to service. This conception of church as servant encompasses and enlarges the idea of the church as the basic sacrament by making Christ present in very visible and tangible ways. And yet, even with this image of church, there is a very real need for balance. While church without service is in fact too narrow a concept, service without church is no different from any social agency. "Service of the community without the Eucharist quickly becomes indistinguishable from humanitarian concerns. Eucharist without service becomes a senseless magical practice."[13]

According to many, this notion of Church as both sacrament and servant is best characterized by the base Christian communities of which have arisen in the so-called Third World. The idea of church as experienced in these communities calls, however, for a radical redefinition of church. Kevin Seasoltz paints a picture of such a church:

> It has to be a suffering servant acknowledging its own need to be saved from sin. Like Christ, the Church must lay down its life for others. Hence, it must be unconcerned about its own prestige and prowess in the world; it must take its agenda, as Christ did, from the poor.[14]

This portrait of church is considerably different from the reality that is now being experienced in many quarters of the world. It is indeed a call for a radical restructuring of the Church. As a result, base communities are often viewed as a threat to the official church structure.

Corresponding to this new perception of church is the subsequent rethinking of the roles of both clergy and laity within the church in general and the liturgy in particular. As a result of Vatican II, the laity were given a place of some significance. The emphasis on active participation of all people, along with such changes as the use of the vernacular and the turning of the altar, served to break down many barriers that had previously existed between the clergy and the laity. Today, base communities give clear witness to this rapidly changing conception of laity and clergy. In light of the number of communities that are unable to celebrate the eucharist because of the lack of an ordained priest, the call for diversified ministry is becoming louder and more distinct. Indeed, in these communities, it is no longer a question of "can we participate?" but rather "to what extent can we go?" The active participation which was sanctioned at Vatican II is rapidly being replaced by a fierce demand on the part of the laity to lead the liturgies. Again, this presents a challenge to church authority.

Despite the attractiveness of the perception of church as depicted by the base communities, however, there remains the crucial question of its relevance to a number of Roman Catholics worldwide. If, as most liberation theologians assert, an authentic Christian community worthy of celebrating the eucharist is comprised of a small number of people who know one another's problems and concerns, this raises a problem for those parishes (such as the vast majority of those in North America, for example) where a large percentage of the congregation do not know one another. Are these not also authentic church communities?

There are, of course, some aspects of base communities which could prove to be of tremendous benefit to large, urban parishes. For those churches which think of themselves in terms of either sacrament or servant, base communities provide a shining example that this must take visible form. All parishes are called to take what is celebrated on Sundays—God's love for humanity—and make this tangible on the other six days of the week. Most notably, this notion of church provides a much needed challenge to the sense of individualism which is so prevalent in much of the so-called First World. Great lessons can be learned regarding the perception of community displayed by these base communities. As Penny Lernoux explains: "While the Third World poor have little in the way of material goods, they have something that the First World has lost in the technical race—a sense of community."[15] While the base community idea of church is simply not adequate as a universal model, it can conceivably act as both a challenge and a paradigm to those already existing models of church, especially those of the First World.

5. The Importance of Response in the Eucharist

For a number of centuries, many Roman Catholics tended to believe that the grace contained in the eucharist was conferred automatically. Although Thomas Aquinas, among others, did assert that the recipient must have a favorable predisposition, the reaction against Luther's justification by grace through faith alone was so strong that many surmised that the eucharist was a mechanical source of grace, independent of the recipient.

In eucharistic theology today, a healthy shift is occurring. From an understanding of the eucharist as a mechanistic bestowal of grace, contemporary theologians are insisting that the eucharist be perceived as a two-way encounter between God and humanity which is comprised of both *offer* and *response*. When the eucharist is understood in terms of interpersonal relationships, as Schillebeeckx does, both elements are equally necessary. Human response to God's invitation becomes a necessary element in that encounter between God and humanity which the eucharist embodies. While Christ is indeed present in the sacrament regardless of individual faith, that presence is nonetheless completely realized only when reciprocated by the individual and the worshipping community.

Only when Christ's presence is both offered and accepted in faith does that presence become intimate.

People can respond in a number of ways to Christ's offer. The act of acceptance can be a matter of an individual's personal response in faith to Christ's offer of himself. On a communal level, Christ's presence in the eucharist is also reciprocated in the faith-filled worship of the believing community. In the eucharistic liturgy, the church responds to Christ's presence offered therein. Moreover, outside the confines of the liturgy, the Church can respond to the encounter with Christ through acts of love and service. Encounters with others in daily life are, therefore, a response to the encounter with Christ in the eucharist.

This dimension of outreach, which is only touched upon by Schillebeeckx, becomes the major form of response for many liberation theologians.[16] According to people such as Boff and Balasuriya, for the complete realization of Christ's presence to occur, a response of outreach and the giving of self to others in service is essential. The eucharist cannot be an end unto itself but must result in a transformation in the daily lives of those who participate in it. Unless this transformation occurs and those who celebrate the eucharist are empowered to serve others, the eucharist remains irrelevant. The emphasis on response as outreach and transformation does not, of course, mean that individual response is not important. Rather, the liberation theologians acknowledge that an inner conversion is a necessary prerequisite to the outer transformation that is concretized in acts of love and service.

Implications

Eucharistic theology is not, and has never been, one isolated area of theology. Any attempt at reinterpreting the eucharist has serious implications and repercussions in many other theological areas. In light of its centrality to the faith of Roman Catholics, this is especially true of the eucharist.

1. Presider of the Eucharist

The progress which has been made in eucharistic theology over the last thirty years is undeniably a great sign of hope for the celebration of the eucharist. Schillebeeckx and those liberation theologians who have explored the eucharist have provided us with firm foundations for making both eucharistic doctrine and the celebration of the eucharist itself meaningful and relevant to ordinary Roman Catholics. Indeed, great strides have been made towards making the eucharist reach its full potential to transform both individuals and society. Unfortunately, this progress is now being thwarted. The role of the presider of the eucharist and the traditional theology of ministry remain a stumbling block. In fact, it is these issues which are becoming the focal point for those who are dealing with questions of the eucharist. Perhaps the best example of this preoccupation is the shift in emphasis in Schillebeeckx' theology. In the 1960's, Schillebeeckx' primary concern was with issues of eucharistic doctrine and the language which he used was highly doctrinal. Beginning in the early 1980's, however, this changed: from matters of eucharistic doctrine, Schillebeeckx shifted his attention to the more pastoral matter of who, considering the crisis in the priesthood, should be allowed to preside at the eucharist.[17]

The concept of ministry is now being questioned primarily because of the number of Christian communities worldwide which are being deprived of the eucharist. For many Catholics, there simply is no ordained priest available to preside over the celebration. Nor does the future look much brighter. Although the exodus from the priesthood has slowed down considerably since the late 1960's and early 1970's, the number of priests continues to decline. For one thing, fewer men than ever before are entering the seminaries. In addition, the average age of those already ordained and active in ministry continues to increase.[18] As a result, more and more communities are left without an ordained minister. While some are administered by another priest, many are left without a weekly eucharistic celebration. Hence, the chances that the crisis in ministry will change on its own seem slim.

Vatican II made the declaration that the eucharist was the source and summit of the entire Christian life. As a result, every Christian community should have the right to a weekly celebration of the eucharist. If this is to be the case, however, wider provision must be made for its celebration. The issue seems clear: if something is not done, eucharistic celebrations will cease to be central to Roman Catholicism. That which is at stake, therefore, is the Catholic church's understanding of itself as a eucharist-centered community.

There are, it seems, two possible solutions to this problem. The first, and less radical, calls for a change in the qualifications and requirements for ordination. This could conceivably take a number of forms. One solution involves those men who have already been ordained but have withdrawn from active ministry, often because they have chosen to marry. Groups such as CORPUS (Catholic Organization for a Renewed Priesthood United for Service) promote a renewed priesthood which would include married priests.[19] For many, the existing crisis in the celebration of the eucharist would be solved by allowing those priests who are married to resume active ministry.

Despite its apparent attractiveness, this alternative could never fully solve the crisis which is now occurring. Most obvious is the fact that the official Church does not, at present, regard this as a viable option. Moreover, the danger exists that this alternative could be no more than a "band-aid" solution to a deeper problem, namely the understanding of ministry. Finally, the possibility exists that such an alternative (if it were to remain static) could ultimately serve to perpetuate an all-male concept of the priesthood. Many female theologians maintain that the answer to the existing crisis in the celebration of the eucharist can be found in the ordination of women. Joan Chittister, for one, adamantly insists that ". . . the whole question of whether the Church is to prefer maleness to Eucharist may well become the central Church issue of the century."[20] While this may indeed be true, the fact remains that the ordination of women continues to be denied by Rome.

Another possibility in solving the crisis in the priesthood would be to make celibacy an optional charism instead of a necessary requirement. This remains a central issue. Mandatory celibacy, it seems, continues to be a prime reason why so few men are entering or staying in the priesthood. Moreover, the issue profoundly affects both the ordination of women and the re-entry of married priests into active ministry. However, if celibacy is in fact the reason that so many communities are being deprived of the eucharist, this is "tantamount to an unlawful violation of the right of the faithful," and, as such, must be reviewed and rethought.[21]

All of the above mentioned possibilities deal with the structure that is already in place. All would retain official, priestly ordination as a requirement for the celebration of the eucharist. A second, more radical, solution to the problem would be to consider alternative practices of celebration in which non-ordained persons would preside over the eucharist. In light of his studies of the development of ministry throughout the history of Christianity, Schillebeeckx adamantly maintains that ministry was never intended to be developed solely around liturgical celebrations. In the early Church, leading the community in worship was only one of many functions. "Ministry is concerned with the leadership of the community: ministers are pioneers, those who inspire the community and serve as models by which the whole community can identify the gospel."[22] Hence, those chosen to lead the worship and preside at the eucharistic celebrations were generally those people who had already proven themselves competent at leading the community.

Over the centuries, however, this whole concept of ministry was altered. The idea of variegated ministries being shared by many members of the community became focused on *one* person who, as leader, would preside over the eucharistic celebrations. Nor was the community any longer given a role in choosing their leader. He was, rather, by virtue of his ordination chosen by the bishop to be the minister who would preside over all aspects of the community into which he was placed. Thus,

> What is clear is that the eucharist was taken out of the hands of the people. And the one who presides at the eucharistic celebration, instead of being able to do so because of a leadership role in the community, can now only do so if "he" is ordained, and even if "he" does not have a leadership role in that community.[23]

In recent years, the call to return to the early Church's understanding of ministry is rapidly growing. In light of the number of Catholics who are being deprived of the eucharist, there is an ever-increasing insistence that the community's right to celebrate the eucharist supplants the requirements of being male, celibate and ordained as is currently demanded of the presider of the eucharist. Accordingly, the community should be given its rightful role of recognizing its leaders and choosing those who will preside at the celebration. In circumstances when there is no priest, then, this non-ordained person would take on the role of presider. It is such a theology of ministry which is currently being sanctioned by Schillebeeckx and put into practice in the celebration of the Lord's Supper in the base communities of the Third World countries.[24]

Such a concept of ministry is, of course, an ideal that is not likely to be condoned by the official Church in the near future. Unfortunately, it is often viewed as a threat, not only to the understanding of priesthood, but also to the entire existing church structure. It is viewed as a menace to the priesthood because it leads to the desacralization of the priesthood. When the role of the community is given primacy, the role of the priest diminishes. Moreover, such alternative practices of celebrating the eucharist are viewed as an assault on the existing church structure insofar as they blatantly indicate the need for a revision of the current structure.[25] It should, therefore, come as no surprise that both *Ministry* and *The Church with the Human Face* were investigated by the doctrinal congregation from 1981-1985 and were found to contain some questionable tenets. What was the main issue? "Schillebeeckx irresponsibly accepts the possibility that, under certain circumstances, someone not officially ordained could preside at the Eucharist."[26]

Although the idea of a non-ordained person presiding at eucharistic celebrations under extra-ordinary circumstances will likely not be officially sanctioned in the near future, indications are that it will eventually prevail:

> . . . in the history of the church there is also a way in which Christians can develop a practice in the church from below, from the grassroots, which for a time can compete with the official practice recognized by the church, but which in its Christian alternative form can eventually nevertheless become the dominant practice

of the church, and finally be sanctioned by the official church . . . This is how things have always been.[27]

As Schillebeeckx demonstrates, and as can be seen in the base communities' celebration of the Lord's Supper, such alternative practices are already taking place and are in fact increasing in number. If history is any indication, these alternative forms will eventually become the dominant practice. The advances that have been made in eucharistic theology are ample evidence that equal progress can be made in the theology of ministry. Indeed, the identity of the Roman Catholic Church as a eucharist-centered community depends on it.

2. Ecumenism

The Second Vatican Council proved to be an enormous catalyst also within the realm of ecumenism. Before the Council, ecumenism was thought of in terms of Protestants "returning" to the one true Church from which they were separated. The *Decree on Ecumenism*, issued in November 1964, drastically changed this perspective. In it, the Council asserted, for the first time in over four hundred years, that Jesus' Spirit is indeed at work in the churches and communities beyond the visible borders of the Roman Catholic Church. The *Decree* upholds this admission to such an extent that it states: "Nor should we forget that whatever is wrought by the grace of the Holy Spirit in the hearts of our separated brethren can contribute to our own edification."[28] To a large extent, the theology of the Protestant churches is identified as authentic and enlightening. Since that time, ecumenical endeavors have been carried over into all areas of theology. This is even true of the core of Roman Catholicism: ". . . eucharistic theology today cannot be done except in an ecumenical framework."[29] Indeed, much of contemporary eucharistic theology has had and will continue to have serious implications for further ecumenical endeavor.

Schillebeeckx' reinterpretation of transubstantiation has certainly been welcomed by other Christian denominations. In regards to transubstantiation, Schillebeeckx has explained that the term was used in the sixteenth century as a "political banner of orthodox faith" which heralded the difference between the Catholic and Protestant views. With little doubt, such an antagonistic understanding of the term has to some extent filtered down to the present day. When the eucharist is reinterpreted in terms of transignification, the term transubstantiation, while both mentioned and retained, is not made primary. By attempting to explain the reality of the real presence in terms other than strictly transubstantiation, then, the barriers which undoubtedly continue to arise when the term is used will be, at least to some extent, overcome. The awareness of the need to find a common language in which to communicate with other Christian churches is thereby acknowledged and reflected.

Besides the issue of language, there are also certain other aspects of Schillebeeckx' reinterpretation which are viewed as ecumenically fruitful. Most notable is the emphasis that is placed on the sign value of the eucharist. In Schillebeeckx' theology, the eucharist is recognized as a sign which realizes what it symbolizes. According to Paul Jersild, a Lutheran scholar, this is promising to ecumenical dialogue insofar as it places the reality of Christ's presence within the context of the symbolic act rather than in the elements of bread and wine alone.[30] Moreover, certain dimensions of Schillebeeckx' theology such as his insistence that the change which occurs is not a physical change, his assertion that Christ is really present in the entire liturgical assembly and, finally, his recognition of the faith response aspect of the interpersonal relationship are perceived as ecumenically favorable elements of eucharistic renewal.[31] All in all, therefore, the understanding of the eucharist as an encounter with Christ has been seen by Protestant theologians as a step forward for ecumenism.

The reinterpretation of the eucharist within the context of liberation theology also has ecumenical ramifications. Again, the language that is used by the liberation theologians in their development of eucharistic theology is not the traditional language of substance and accidents which often proved to be antagonistic in ecumenical endeavor. As a result, ecumenical dialogue will most definitely be facilitated.

Most important, however, is the fact that many groups that may not agree about doctrine are nonetheless discovering that they are being brought together in their common work for justice. Doctrine is not the foremost concern for most of these theologians. Rather, of greatest importance is the human situation in which that doctrine is lived. In the celebration of the Lord's Supper, therefore, people are celebrating together in the Spirit of Jesus, regardless of doctrinal differences which may be a cause of division.

Arising from such ecumenical celebrations is the issue once again of ministry. The question arises: if Rome does not consider these celebrations which are presided by a non-ordained person to be a celebration of the eucharist, what is to be said of those celebrations led by Protestant ministers who have not received the sacrament of orders in the Catholic Church? Are these not to be considered authentic, albeit incomplete, eucharistic celebrations?[32] And, if they are considered authentic, then ". . . what holds for Protestant celebrations should hold *a fortiori* for the celebrations of Catholic lay co-ordinators."[33] Thus, the understanding of ministry has tremendous ramifications for ecumenical dialogue.

3. Church Authority

More often than not, attempts at eucharistic reinterpretation have, at least to some extent, been viewed as deviations from traditional church doctrine. The renewal of eucharistic theology by Schillebeeckx and the liberation theologians, have in fact been refuted by Vatican documents. Both *Mysterium Fidei* and the *Instruction on Certain Aspects of Liberation Theology* accuse these theologians of deviating away from traditional orthodox teaching on the eucharist. I would argue, however, that both reinterpretations are more an expansion of, rather than a deviation from, traditional doctrine. Schillebeeckx insists that transubstantiation be retained in the doctrine of the eucharist. Transignification, he maintains, should not replace transubstantiation, but should be used to enhance that part of transubstantiation—the personal, human dimension—which for so long had been neglected. The liberation theologians also retain transubstantiation. Transubstantiation is taken for granted in their reinterpretation insofar as they insist that the transformation of life occurs because it is *really* Christ who, in the eucharist, calls us to be converted. While at the same time retaining traditional doctrine, contemporary eucharistic theologians seek to go beyond the doctrine to make it more meaningful for those who celebrate and are transformed by the eucharist.

Be this as it may, there is undoubtedly tension between the advocates eucharistic renewal and the official church. This tension stems, I would suggest, from a distortion on the part of the official church about the meaning of unity. The call in both *Mysterium Fidei* and the *Instruction* has been a demand for unity. At times, however, the call for unity has appears to be more of a demand for uniformity.

In terms of liturgical celebrations, for example, Vatican II called for plurality which, while retaining unity, would also take into account regional and even congregational diversities.[34] Often, however, such religious inculturation is difficult. In many Third World countries, bread and wine are not a daily fare. Phillippe Rouillard questions their use in eucharistic celebrations:

> Bread and wine are foreign words for many Christians of Africa and the Far East who do not use them as food and drink. One can very legitimately wonder whether it is in accord with Christ's intention to employ signs which in these regions really do not signify anything and if it would not be better to adopt instead some food and beverage in use in the region in question.[35]

Unfortunately, in the name of unity, Rome has declared that bread and wine are to be the matter of the eucharist.

Likewise, mandatory clerical celibacy is being demanded of the presider of the eucharist by the official church authorities. Again, this does not take into account the traditions and conventions of many Third World people.

> . . . in many tribal cultures celibacy is not regarded as an authentic human value . . . there will never be enough priests to celebrate the Eucharist because few tribal people will sacrifice their standing in the community to become ordained.[36]

In many cases, it seems that the demand for uniformity of practice has surpassed Vatican II's call for plurality.

Increasingly, many Catholics are insisting that the pluralism advocated by Vatican II be put into practice. As a result, they are asking the official church for the freedom to try new methods of worship which would be better suited to their own situations. Unity, they insist, takes into consideration the diversity of people. "Uniformity is a caricature of genuine unity, which depends on a respect for diversity."[37] Unity, they contend, does not necessarily demand uniformity.

This criticism of the official church's position is in no way meant to imply that there is nothing good happening at the official level. The *Constitution on the Sacred Liturgy* at Vatican II, certain aspects of the encyclical *Mysterium Fidei* and the work done at the 41st Eucharistic Congress on the theme of the eucharist and human hunger are ample evidence that some progress is being made at the official level. Such changes, however, are often inadequate and slow in providing answers to urgent problems. Instead of working to provide solutions to such problems as the lack of ordained presiders for the eucharistic celebrations, the official church for the most part seems content to reiterate the teaching that has been passed down through the centuries. Dissatisfied with this seeming indifference on Rome's part, many theologians are now insisting that "theology also has the mission of seeking out adequate answers to new and urgent problems, using the resources of the *depositum fidei*."[38] It is precisely this "seeking out of adequate answers" that is the fundamental goal of contemporary eucharistic theologians.

The ideal here would be a collaborative effort on the part of both the official church on one side and the theologians and people on the other. Unfortunately, this does not seem to be happening. To the contrary, that which appears to be emerging are two separate tracks. On the one hand, there are those theologians who, in recognition of the problems facing contemporary eucharistic theology, are attempting to expand the traditional understanding of the eucharist in order to make it meaningful for those who participate in the celebration. Also included in this group are those Roman Catholics who participate in such liturgical celebrations as the Lord's Supper where there is no ordained minister and who, despite Rome's insistence on the conditions of ordination, still consider these to be authentic eucharistic celebrations. To say that this group is oblivious of the official church's position is a wrong choice of words. They well know the persecution that their theologians are undergoing because of their stances. Be this as it may, however, the fact that they continue to celebrate these "illegal deviations" proves that these people intend to proceed in developing authentic and meaningful celebrations of the eucharist, regardless of Rome's dissatisfaction.

On the other side is the position taken by the official church. In addition to the direct criticism and rejection of the work of the theologians who are attempting to reinterpret the doctrine of the eucharist, there is also some evidence that the official church does not take into account the advances that have been made in the area of eucharistic theology over the past thirty years. The proposed *Catechism for the Universal Church* is a good example: "[It] is couched in terms which have been bypassed over the last thirty years. To go back and talk about the issues of the late eighties in the language of the fifties is not an accident. It is an attempt to say that all that happened in between doesn't count."[39]

Nowhere is this fact more evident that in the section on the eucharist. Those reviewing the document maintain that the major flaw is the statement that the eucharist is not a meal. This meal aspect, as we have seen, is one of the major emphases in eucharistic theology today. Likewise, other significant aspects of the eucharistic reinterpretation have been downplayed or ignored altogether in the *Catechism.* "The catechism downplays the communal aspects of the eucharist. The document makes few references to the Church as People of God."[40] It would appear, therefore, that the official church is satisfied with simply repeating the eucharistic theology put forth four hundred years ago at the Council of Trent without taking into account the progress made at and since the Second Vatican Council.

This is not meant to imply that modern attempts at eucharistic renewal are totally correct while the church's stance against them is totally incorrect. Certainly, there are problems which still have to be worked out in much of contemporary eucharistic theology. Undoubtedly, it is probably subject, as is all of theology, to a certain amount of distortion. The official church is justified, therefore, in proceeding with some degree of caution. However, as we have seen, the trend appears to be more than reluctance on the official church's part. Rather, it appears to be an indifference to the cries of the people. As a result, the gulf between the two positions continues to widen.

What the outcome will be of these two divergent tracks of theology remains to be seen. Perhaps the two will grow insurmountably apart, resulting in a split within the church. The hope remains, however, that these so-called "illegal deviations" will eventually be sanctioned by the official church. It is to be desired that the changes in eucharistic theology and practice which have occurred since the Second Vatican Council and which are at the moment taking place outside the limits of the official church will one day be accepted as authentic and meaningful expressions of the eucharist celebrated in the Spirit of Jesus.

Discussion Questions

1. Despite the advances which have been made in eucharistic theology by Schillebeeckx, Balasuriya, Boff and others, why does the celebration of the eucharist remain in crisis?

2. What is meant by the statement: "If authentically celebrated, the eucharist has the potential to transform individual lives and all of society"? What further changes are necessary for this to occur at least to some extent within your own situation?

3. One example of making the celebration of the eucharist grounded in reality and applicable to a specific time and situation is to allow indigenous people to celebrate the eucharist with elements which are staples for them rather than insisting on bread and wine. Give two more possible ways in which the eucharist could be made applicable to a specific time and situation.

4. List concrete examples which point to the fact that the sign value of the eucharist as a meal is being restored.

5. Describe the renewed understanding and role of the community in regards to the celebration of the eucharist. Is this understanding of community plausible for your situation? Explain.

6. Which image of church is most predominant in your situation? How has it been implemented?

7. Five areas of common ground have been listed. Can you think of others which point the way for the future of eucharistic theology?

8. Out of the two possible solutions which have been given for solving the crisis of ministry, which do you feel is most attractive? Most plausible? Why?

9. Are there any practical examples of the influence of ecumenism on the celebration of the eucharist in your own situation? What are they?

10. "Unity does not necessarily demand uniformity." Explain this statement within the context of the celebration of the eucharist.

11. What do you think the outcome will be of the two divergent tracks of eucharistic theology? Explain.

12. What do you think the future holds for the celebration of the eucharist? Explain.

Endnotes

Introduction

1. Throughout the course of this book, I will refer to the eucharist with a lower case "e." This is a deliberate attempt on my part to avoid the objectification of the term. It is my contention that when eucharist is spelled with an upper case "E," the emphasis tends to be put on the bread and wine as *objects* of worship rather than the entire celebration as an *action* of worship.

2. Joseph Martos. *Doors to the Sacred: A Historical Introduction to Sacraments in the Catholic Church*. (Garden City, New York: Image Books, 1982), p. 248.

3. Thomas Aquinas. *Summa Theologiae*. (Latin text and English translation; introductions, notes, appendices, glossaries. Blackfriars. London: Eyre and Spottiswoode; N.Y.: McGraw-Hill Book Co., 1964.) (Hereinafter referred to as *ST*). III, 83,6.

4. Thomas Bokenkotter. *A Concise History of the Catholic Church*. (Garden City, N.Y.: Image Books, 1979), p. 156.

5. *Ibid*, p. 424.

Chapter One

1. As Allan McDonald attests, Berengar "completed rather than started a long line of spiritual teachers who held views similar to his own." Allan McDonald. *Berengar and the Reform of Sacramental Doctrine*. (Merrick, New York: Richwood Publishing Company, 1977), p. 227.

2. This unclarity is due in no little part to the fact that the majority of Berengar's works were destroyed and the one which did survive was not discovered until seven centuries later. As a result, "it has largely been from quotations supplied by his opponents that later scholars have been obliged to reconstruct Berengar's thought." Jaroslav Pelikan. *The Growth of Medieval Theology (600-1300)*. (Chicago: University of Chicago Press, 1978), p. 187.

3. As quoted in K.M. Purday. "Berengar and the Use of the Word *Substantia*." *The Downside Review*. (Volume 91. Number 303. April 1973.), pp. 101-108.

4. I am referring at this point to Allan McDonald. McDonald's work, although dated, seems to be the authority on the Berengarian controversy: all other scholars refer to this work.

5. McDonald, p. 284.

6. *Ibid*, p. 361.

7. *Ibid*, p. 362.

8. *Ibid*, p. 259.

9. Gustave Martelet. *The Risen Christ and the Eucharistic World*. (New York: Seabury Press, 1976), p. 133.

10. McDonald, p. 261.

11. *Ibid*, p. 315.

12. Justo Gonzalez. *A History of Christian Thought*. (Nashville: Abingdon Press, 1971), p. 151.

13. McDonald, p. 285.

14. Pelikan, p. 198.

15. Joseph M. Powers. *Eucharistic Theology*. (New York: Herder and Herder, 1967), p. 29.

16. It is necessary to note at this point that the metaphysical theory of substance and accidents had not yet been standardized. Berengar in fact did not even use the term "accidents" in connection with "substance" but referred rather to the qualities of an object. K. Purday notes this fact and goes on to explain that the term "substance" for Berengar referred to the entire physical structure of a thing. Purday, pp. 104-106.

17. McDonald, p. 256.

18. Purday, p. 101.

19. McDonald, p. 256.

20. McDonald, p. 278-279.

21. *Ibid*, p. 280.

22. *Ibid*, p. 281.

23. Purday, p. 101.

24. Oath of 1059 as quoted in McDonald, p. 130.

25. McDonald, p. 296.

26. *Ibid*, p. 296.

27. Gonzalez, p. 152.

28. McDonald, p. 295.

29. Purday, p. 103.

30. Gonzalez, p. 153.

31. McDonald, p. 347.

32. Denzinger. *The Sources of Catholic Dogma*. (London: B. Herder Book Co.,1957),# 355. (Hereinafter referred to as *DS* #)

33. Purday, p. 103.

34. Pelikan, p. 203.

35. McDonald, p. 263.

36. Richard McBrien. *Catholicism*. (San Francisco: Harper and Row, 1981), p. 51.

37. Bokenkotter, p. 174.

38. *ST*, III, 75, 2 ad 2.

39. *Ibid*, III, 79, 7 ad 1.

40. J. de Baciocchi. *L'Eucharistie*. (Tournai, Belgium: Desclee and Co., 1961), p. 82.

41. *ST* III, 75, 1.

42. *ST*, III, 74, 4. By the time Thomas was writing the *Summa*, transubstantiation had already been made the official dogma of the Roman Catholic Church. The Fourth Lateran Council in 1215 had declared: "Jesus Christ, whose body and blood are truly contained in the sacrament of the altar under the species of bread and wine, the bread changed into His Body by the divine power of transubstantiation, and the wine into His Blood . . . ," *DS* #430.

43. As Yves de Montcheil explains: "la conversion de la substance du pain est le seul moyen de rendre le Christ réelement présente dans l'Eucharistie." in "La raison de la permanence du Christ sous les espèces eucharistiques d'après Bon-

aventure et Thomas." *Mélanges Théologiques: Série Théologie, n. 9.* (Paris: Editions du Cerf, 1946), p. 81.

44. *ST* III, 80, 1 ad 1. As well, related to this discussion of the fact of the real presence is Thomas' assertion of the permanence of the real presence after consecration. In asserting that all people receive Christ's body and blood, Thomas insisted that after consecration Christ's body remained under the species of the bread as long as the bread remained. This assertion may be seen as further proof of the reality of Christ's presence in the eucharist.

45. *ST*, III, 82, 5.

46. Part of Thomas' explanation of the mode of the real presence included the assertion that the whole Christ was present under each and every part of the species: "You are to think then of the whole Christ as being under each and every part of the appearances of the bread." *ST* III, 76, 3.

47. *ST* III, 75, 5. Accidents by this time was a normal part of the vocabulary of eucharistic doctrine. Thomas does, however, also use the term species—cf. for example *ST* III, 80, 3. Accidents, the editor of the *Summa* explains, refers to "the quantity, quality and all the other extra-substantial forms that affect a substance." *ST* Vol. LVIII, p. 74. It is important to note, however, that "Thomas did not raise the tools of substance and accidents—Aristotelian precisions—to the level of a dogma.," p. 299. Thus, while making use of the terms of Aristotelian philosophy, Thomas did not make them part of the doctrine of transubstantiation itself.

48. *ST* III, 77, 7.

49. *Ibid*, III, 75, 1 ad 2 and ad 3.

50. *Ibid*, III, 75, 1.

51. *Ibid*, III, 80, 1.

52. *ST* 80, 3.: "So long as the species last, Christ's body does not cease to be under them." 53. *Ibid*, III, 80, 4.

54. *Ibid*, III, 80, 1.

55. *ST* III, 75, 1 ad 1. This concept of spiritual eating, as K. McDonnell observes, did not exclude a real eating but simply a material eating. In defence of Augustine's statement "You will not be eating this body which you see," Thomas asserted that: "He does not intend to exclude the reality of Christ's body; what he does rule out is that they would eat it under the same form in which they were looking at it." III, 75,1 ad 1. Thomas' exposition of spiritual eating, then, while ensuring a belief in Christ's real presence in the sacrament, excluded a capharnaitic understanding of that presence. Hence, McDonnell concludes, by maintaining a distinction between sacramental and spiritual eating, Thomas guarded against "a species of sacramental realism which is in fact not at all sacramental but quite clearly crude religious materialism." Kilian McDonnell. *John Calvin, the Church and the Eucharist.* (Princeton, N.J.: Princeton University Press, 1967), p. 306.

56. *ST*, III, 79, 3.

57. *ST*, III, 79, 6.

58. *Ibid*, III, 73, 3.

59. Francis Clarke. *Eucharistic Sacrifice and the Reformation.* (London: Darton, Longman and Todd, Ltd., 1960), p. 79.

60. *ST* III, 83, 1.

61. *Ibid*, III, 73, 5 ad 2.

62. John Hughes. "Eucharistic Sacrifice: Transcending the Reformation Deadlock." *Worship.* Volume 43. Number 9. P. 541. "Sacrifices properly speaking occur when something is done with regard to a thing offered to God: as when animals are killed, when bread is broken, and eaten and blessed." As Colman O'Neill observes, Thomas did not ever offer an explicit explanation of the intricate relationship between the consecration and the sacrifice of the Mass. However, O'Neill continues this observation with the statement that "Abbot Vonier's sacrament-sacrifice theory, according to which the double consecration symbolizes and effects sacramentally the Passion of Christ, appears to interpret faithfully his theology." Colman O'Neill. "The Role of the Recipient and Sacramental Signification." *Thomist.* Volume 21. 1958. P. 523. Likewise, Nicholas Gihr, when considering the way in which Christ's body and blood are offered in the eucharist, interprets Thomas' understanding as follows: "This consists in the mystical shedding of blood, that is, in the separate consecration of the bread and wine into the body and blood of Christ. The separate species, under which Christ's body and blood are rendered present by virtue of the words of consecration, that is, mystically immolated, are symbols of the violent and bloody death of Christ on the cross." Nicholas Gihr. *The Holy Sacrifice of the Mass.* (St. Louis: B. Herder Book Co., 1949), p. 138.

63. *ST* III, 76, 2 ad 1.

64. It was, the editor of the *Summa* maintains, in order to stress the real identification of the sacrifice of the cross and the sacrifice of the Mass that Thomas preferred the more explicative term of *immolatio*, rather than *sacrificium*. *ST* Volume LIX. P. 133.

65. *ST* III, 77, 7 ad 3.

66. *Ibid,* III, 82, 5.

67. *Ibid* III, 83, 1.

68. *Ibid* III, 75, 5 ad 3.

69. De Baciocchi, p. 47.

70. *ST* III, 79, 7.

71. *Ibid* III, 79, 5.

72. *Ibid* III, 77, 7.

73. *Ibid* III, 78, 3 ad 7.

74. *Ibid* III, 79, 1. It is necessary to recognize that while Thomas did assert that the Mass as sacrifice was effective not only for those who consecrated the eucharist, but for those who received as well as for those for whom it was offered (III, 79, 5), he did nevertheless continue to affirm the need for faith in Christ's Passion. In III, 79, 7 ad 2, he declared that "this sacrifice, which is a memorial of the Lord's passion, has no effect save on those who are united to the sacrament through faith and charity." Hence, despite the fact that the eucharist, as the sacrifice of Christ, need not be received in order to be efficacious, faith in that which was re-presented and from which it gained its power was a necessary element in the appropriation of its grace.

75. McDonnell, p. 327.

76. Powers, p. 40.

77. Jaroslav Pelikan. *Reformation of Church and Dogma (1300-1700).* (Chicago: University of Chicago Press, 1984), p. 298.

78. An important point to note here is that, as Schillebeeckx explains, Trent did not deal with the manifold presences of Christ in the liturgy. The concern was not with the different forms of Christ's real presence, but with the safeguarding of the significance of his presence in the eucharist. Edward Schillebeeckx. *The Eucharist.* (N.Y.: Sheed and Ward, 1968), p. 42.

79. Although these Reformers agreed that the words of institution were not to be taken literally, they did not agree on what the interpretation should be. Zwingli, for example, used the interpretation set forth by Cornelius Hoen who suggested that the verb "to be" is often used in the Bible in a metaphorical sense, as when Jesus calls himself the true vine, the resurrection and the life, and the bread of life. As in these contexts, when Jesus obviously used the verb "to be" in the sense of "to signify," so in the words of institution "This is my body" should be understood as "This signifies" or "This represents" my body. Oecolampadius' interpretation was close to that of Zwingli; the bread and wine were to be seen as a figure or sign of the body and blood of Christ. Schwenckfeld, on the other hand, did not equate "to be" with "to signify," but proposed that the words of institution should instead be interpreted to mean, "Take and eat. My body given for you is this." viz. a spiritual food." (*LW* 37:40). Karlstadt, finally, proposed that when Christ said "This is my body," he was pointing to himself and not, therefore, to the bread and wine. All of the above did, however, agree that a symbolic interpretation was the only proper one. Cf. also David Steinmetz. "Scripture and the Lord's Supper in Luther's Theology." *Interpretation.* Vol. 37. No. 3. July 1983. pp. 225ff.

80. *DS*, #883.

81. *Ibid,* #876.

82. *Ibid.*

83. DeBaciocchi, p. 81.

84. *DS*, #876.

85. *Ibid,* #886.

86. As Edward Schillebeeckx concludes: "This insistence of the Tridentine dogma on the *lasting* character of Christ's real presence in the eucharist points to the special and distinctive reality of this particular presence." Schillebeeckx, p. 44.

87. In *The Babylonian Captivity of the Church,* Luther expressed this concern: "My one concern at present is to remove all scruples of conscience, so that no one may fear being called a heretic." Martin Luther. *Luther's Works.* (Hereinafter referred to as *LW*) Vol 36. Ed. by Helmut T. Lehmenn. (Philadelphia: Fortress Press, 1951), p. 30.

88. *LW* 36:31.

89. *DS,*#877.

90. *Ibid,* #884.

91. *Ibid,* #877.

92. Schillebeeckx, p. 42.

93. Pelikan, p. 299.

94. Schillebeeckx, p. 41.

95. Schillebeeckx is a notable exception. In response to claims that the Council avoided using the term "accidents" purposely in order to disassociate itself from the Aristotelian philosophical framework, Schillebeeckx insists both that species and accident were synonymous terms for the Fathers, and also

that they themselves were Aristotelian scholastics. Hence, while he does agree that the Council was not concerned with settling scholastic disputes between Catholic theologians, he does emphatically maintain that the Fathers were not trying to disassociate themselves from a certain framework. Cf. pp. 54-56.

96. Thomas Ambrogi. "Contemporary Roman Catholic Theology of the Eucharistic Sacrifice: Sacramental Reality, Sign and Presence," in *Lutherans and Catholics in Dialogue, I-III.* Ed. by Paul C. Empie and T. Austin Murphy. (Minneapolis: Augsburg Publishing House, 1974), p. 157.

97. "The sense is general but fixed and means the profound fundament of a thing." McDonnell, p. 301.

98. Gustave Martelet. *The Risen Christ and the Eucharistic World.* (N.Y.: Seabury Press, 1976), p. 106.

99. "The fundamental element of the scholastic doctrine of transubstantiation, the complete change of substance, should be upheld, not on any merely philosophical ground, but as corresponding with the full faith of the Church in the real presence." D. J. B. Hawkins. "Reflections on transubstantiation." *The Downside Review.* Vol. 80. 1962. p. 315.

100. LW 37: 370-371. While Luther did retain the idea that the sacrifice of Christ was present in the eucharist insofar as His body and blood, given in that one sacrifice of Calvary, were also present, he nonetheless rejected the conception of the Roman Catholic priesthood which claimed to have inherited the power to enact Christ's sacrifice in the Mass. Furthermore, Luther rejected the Roman Catholic understanding of the Mass, not merely as a result of the abuses that had arisen around the doctrine of sacrifice, but also on the grounds that it had distorted the true meaning of the eucharist. That is, he insisted that the Mass had come to be understood as a means to an end and a way to appease God, rather than as a testament by which Christ had bequeathed to His heirs the inheritance of the forgiveness of sin. (*LW* 35:86-87). It was, then, on this basis that Luther rejected the Roman Catholic doctrine of the sacrifice of the Mass.

101. Hughes, p.536.

102. *DS, #948.*

103. *DS, #939.*

104. It is important to note that there was some disagreement on this point. Hubert Jedin maintains that some doubt was expressed not only about the sacrificial nature of the Lord's Supper but especially about the transfer of the power to sacrifice Christ to the apostles. In view of the fact that this doubt was expressed by a minority, however, the two assertions became part of the official doctrine of the sacrifice of the Mass. Hubert Jedin. *Crisis and Closure of the Council of Trent: A Retrospective View from the Second Vatican Council.* (London: Sheed and Ward, 1967), p. 70.

105. Pelikan, p. 300. Also cf. Canon four: "If anyone says that blasphemy is cast upon the most holy sacrifice of Christ consummated on the Cross through the sacrifice of the Mass, or that by it He is disparaged: let him be anathema." *DS, #951.*

106. *DS, #940.* Nicholas Gihr succinctly sums up this idea with the following affirmation: "Between the two there exists the most perfect unity so far as we consider the victim and the priest; for it is Christ who offers upon the

altar His body and His blood, consequently the same gift which He once offered on the Cross.," p. 139.

107. Ambrogi, p . 152.

108. *DS,* # 938.

109. Perhaps this was not the only reason for the Fathers' assertion that the Mass was a propitiatory sacrifice. John Hughes maintains that the Fathers understood the representation as a mental recalling of Calvary on the part of the worshippers, as did the Reformers. "Hence the Catholic apologists of the Reformation period felt it necessary to go beyond the notion of representation, which for them did not safeguard the truth that the mass was a true sacrifice." p. 536. However, I would suggest that the Fathers may well have understood "representation" in the more forceful sense of making present Christ's sacrifice, but, in light of the fact that the Reformers did not understand it in that sense, went on to declare that the Mass was a propitiatory sacrifice.

110. *DS,* #940.

111. *Ibid,* #940.

Chapter Two

1. Josef Jungmann. *Commentary on the Documents of Vatican II.* Ed. Herbert Vorgrimler (N.Y.: Herder and Herder, 1967), p. 20.

2. This is not to say that the need for authentic reform was not felt before the twentieth century. To the contrary, seventeenth century France and eighteenth century Germany in particular called for a renewal of liturgy. However, these centuries are not of particular importance to this study because, as Jungmann points out, "these earlier attempts at reform did not lead to any lasting success," p. 2.

3. Pope Pius XII. *Mediator Dei.* in *The Papal Encyclicals in their Historical Context.* Ed. Anne Fremantle. (N.Y.: New American Library, 1956), p. 287.

4. Adrian Hastings. *A Concise Guide to the Documents of the Second Vatican Council.* (London: Darton, Longmann and Todd, 1968), p. 129.

5. Pope Pius XII, p. 286.

6. *Ibid,* p. 287.

7. Jungmann, p. 8.

8. "Constitution on the Sacred Liturgy." in *The Documents of Vatican II.* Ed. Walter M. Abbott. (New Jersey: New Century Publishers, 1966), Article 1. (Hereinafter referred to as *CSL.*)

9. Even in *The Roman Catechism,* however, the exposition on the doctrine of the eucharist is for the most part a repetition of that which was established at the Council of Trent.

10. *CSL,* Art. 14.

11. Jungmann, p. 17.

12. *Documents on the Liturgy, 1963-1979: Conciliar, Papal and Curial Texts.* (Hereinafter referred to as *DOL.*) (Collegeville, Minnesota: The Liturgical Press, 1982), 189 #1325.

13. *CSL,* Art. 14.

14. *CSL,* Art. 11.

15. It is important to acknowledge the new vision of the Church which is developed in the Council documents. In the *Dogmatic Constitution on the Church*, the Church is referred to primarily as the Pilgrim People of God. This concept of church, as opposed to the notion of the church as *the* institution of salvation has numerous repercussions. The Church is no longer identified with the Kingdom of God on earth, but is understood as working towards that end. The Church as pilgrim people is subject to deviations and imperfections, since it has not yet reached the end of the pilgrimage. Likewise, the Church is deeply involved in, rather than apart from history. George Lindbeck. *The Future of Roman Catholic Theology: Vatican II—The Catalyst for Change*. (Philadelphia: Fortress Press, 1970), pp. 33-34.

16. "Dogmatic Constitution on the Church" in *The Documents of Vatican II*. Ed. Walter M. Abbot (New Jersey: New Century Publishers, 1966). Articles 31 & 32.

17. Joseph Cordeiro. "The Liturgy Constitution." in *Vatican II Revisited by those who were there*. Ed. Alberic Stacpoole. (Minneapolis: Winston Press, 1986), p. 189.

18. *CSL*, Art. 26.

19. *Ibid*, Art. 27.

20. Lindbeck, p. 72.

21. Everett Diederich. "Reflections on post-conciliar shifts in eucharistic faith and practice." *Communio (US)*. Vol. 12. Summer 1985. P. 226.

22. *CSL*, Art.8.

23. Raymond B. Fullam. *Exploring Vatican II: Christian Living Today and Tomorrow*. (Montreal: Palm Publishers, 1969),p. 224.

24. *CSL*, Art. 7.

25. Joseph Powers. "Eucharist: Symbol of Freedom and Community." in *Christian Spirituality in the United States*. Ed. F. Eigo. 1978. p. 189-197.

26. Joseph Powers. "Food for Wayfarers." *New Catholic World*. January-February 1986. p. 40.

27. Pope Paul VI. *Mysterium Fidei*. In *The Papal Encyclicals: 1958-1981*. Ed. Claudia Carlen. (McGrath Publishing House, 1981), #39.

28. Hastings, p. 122.

29. *DOL* 177 #1223.

30. *Eucharisticum Mysterium*. In *Vatican II: The Conciliar and Post-Conciliar Documents*. Ed. Austin Flannery. (Wilmington, Delaware: Scholarly Resources Inc., 1975), p. 133.

31. Hastings, p. 123.

32. *CSL*, Art. 61.

33. *Ibid*, Art. 33.

34. Liam Walsh. "The Sacraments and Sacramentals." in *Vatican II: Liturgical Constitution*. Ed. Austin Flannery. (Dublin; Scepter Books, 1964), p. 45.

35. *CSL*, Art. 50.

36. *Ibid*, Art. 23.

37. A. Verheul. *Introduction to the Liturgy*. (Collegeville, Minnesota: The Liturgical Press, 1968), p. 33.

38. *CSL*, Art. 24.

39. *Ibid*, Art. 52.

40. Jungmann, p. 39.

41. *CSL*, Art. 30.

42. *Ibid*, Art. 36,#2.

43. Gary MacEoin. *What Happened at Rome? The Council and its Implications for the Modern World*. (N.Y.: Echo Book, 1967), p. 91. Also cf. *CSL* Art. 36, #3: "It is for the competent territorial ecclesiastical authority mentioned in Article 22, #2 to decide whether, and to what extent, the vernacular language is to be used according to these norms; their decrees are to be approved, that is, confirmed, by the Apostolic See."

44. MacEoin, pp. 93-94.

45. Hastings, pp. 129-130.

46. *CSL*, Art. 55.

47. Hastings, p. 131.

48. Louis Bouyer. *The Liturgy Revived: A Doctrinal Commentary of the Conciliar Constitution on the Liturgy*. (Notre Dame, Indiana: University of Notre Dame Press, 1964), p. 67.

Chapter Three

1. It must be emphasized that this train of thought had been circulating for a number of years prior to the Second Vatican Council. In fact, certain elements—in particular, the expanded notion of sacrament—greatly influenced Vatican II documents. "The years 1964 and 1965 marked the beginning of a new phase in the reinterpretation of Christ's real presence. By this, I mean that it was then that the new ideas which had been developed in different countries, especially during the ten years following the publication of *Humani Generis* in 1950, became widely known in the Church as a whole." In Edward Schillebeeckx. *The Eucharist*. (N.Y.: Sheed and Ward, 1968), p. 114.

2. Edward Schillebeeckx. "Transubstantiation, Transfinalization, Transfiguration." *Worship*. Vol. 40. No. 6. 1966. p. 325.

3. Kenan Osborne cites a number of theologians who were precursors of this work even before World War II: L. Billot, M. de la Taille, Odo Casels, A. Vonier, J. Ternus, A. Maltha, and F. Unterkircher. Cf. Kenan Osborne, "Contemporary Understandings of the Eucharist: A Survey of Catholic Thinking," *Journal of Ecumenical Studies*. Vol. 13. No. 2. Spring 1979. p. 4.

   As well, Edward Kilmartin adds to the list by citing Yves de Montcheuil as the first to use the term 'transfinalization.' Cf. E.J. Kilmartin. "Sacramental Theology; The Eucharist in Recent Literature." *Theological Studies*. Vol. 32. June 1971. p. 234.

4. Schillebeeckx, 1968, pp. 94-106. Kenan Osborne adds to these five by including the rise of historical consciousness and philosophical pluralism. Osborne, 1979, p. 6.

5. *Ibid*, p. 94. For the purposes of this book, we will use only Selvaggi and Columbo in order to explain the issue. This is not to say that they were the only two involved in the controversy. Cf., for example, Cyril Vollert's excellent overview: "The Eucharist: Controversy on Transubstantiation." *Theological Studies*. Vol. 22. 1961.

6. "If . . . bread is now to be thought of as consisting of atoms and molecules, instead of as a sole entity, then one must say that transubstantiation involves the conversion of the substance of each of the atoms, molecules, and mesons

into the substance of the body of Christ. Richard G. Cipolla. "Selvaggi Revisited: Transubstantiation and Contemporary Science." *Theological Studies.* Vol. 35. No. 4. December 1974. p. 668.

7. Vollert, 1961, p. 394. Vollert is quick to point out that Selvaggi did in fact make a distinction: if by physical change, one was referring to a real change between two real physical terms, transubstantiation is a physical change. But "if by physical change we mean, in the language of modern physics, a change brought about by a series of physical operations, evidently transubstantiation is not a physical change. Although the substance of bread is no longer present under the species after the consecration, it is impossible to verify experimentally the change that has occurred since all experimentation has as immediate object the species of properties, not the substance, which is the object of judgement."

8. Cipolla, 1974, p. 669.

9. Vollert, 1961, p. 397.

10. Cipolla, 1974, p. 670.

11. Both Cipolla and Osborne state that the argument was long and rather obscure.

12. Osborne, 1979, p. 5.

13. Schillebeeckx, 1968, pp. 96-100.

14. Osborne, 1979, p. 5.

15. Schillebeeckx, 1968, p. 100. Joseph Powers gives a great example of this: "Canvas and oil, drafting pens and paper, paper and ink are robbed of their physical reality in their assumption into the act of conveying insight, intelligence or emotion from one person to others. They remain themselves physically, it is true, and they can be subjected to physical examination and be found to be paper, canvas, oil and so on. But their existential reality in the human sign-act is that of the symbolic instrument which literally and effectively incarnating and expressing that reality to man's world." Joseph Powers. *Eucharistic Theology.* (N.Y.: Herder and Herder, 1967), pp. 85-86.

16. That which is on the altar are sacramental signs which ". . . sont réelement le moyen par lequel s'exprime et s'accomplit le don total et véritable, personnel et corporel, du seigneur à l'Eglise." J. De. Baciocchi. "Présence eucharistique et transsubstantiation." *Irénikon.* Vol. 32. 1959. p. 148.

17. *Ibid,* p. 150. Transubstantiation is necessary, de Baciocchi maintained, in order to discard several wrong ideas of what occurs at the eucharistic change. First, it dismisses the notion that what occurs at the consecration is a complete transmutation in the area of chemical reactions, since nothing changes on either the experiential or the scientific level. As well, transubstantiation rejects the idea that the change which occurs is a purely relative change; that is, that the bread itself is not modified at any level, but merely made use of in a different way. The dogma also repudiates the position—consubstantiation—which states that the bread remains bread and, at the same time, becomes the body of Christ. Lastly, transubstantiation reacts against the theory that the bread is made up of two separate entities—an outer membrane that can relate to the senses and an inner core or substance. At consecration, according to this position, only the bread's outer stratum remains, while the inner kernel disappears and is replaced by Christ's body and blood.

18. *Ibid*, pp. 155-158.

19. Vollert, 1961, p. 418.

20. Schillebeeckx, 1968, p. 102.

21. "... les définitions eucharistiques en matière eucharistique du XIe au XVIe siècle aient attribué au terme "substantia" un sens technique spécial et nouveau. Elles ont repris ce mot en un sens tres général, quoique très ferme, de réalité profonde, solide, fondamentale des choses." G. Ghysens. "Présence réele et transsubstantiation dans les définitions de l'Eglise Catholique." *Irénikon*. Vol 32. 1959. p. 429.

22. Schillebeeckx, 1968, p. 102.

23. Edward J. Kilmartin. "Christ's Presence in the Liturgy." in *Bread from Heaven*. Ed. Paul Bernier. (N.Y.: Paulist Press, 1977), p. 105.

24. Everett Diederich. "The unfolding presence of Christ in the Mass." *Communio (US)*. Winter 1978. p. 336.

25. Schillebeeckx, 1968, p. 104.

26. *Ibid*, p. 105.

27. F.J. Leenhardt. "This is my Body." *Ecumenical Studies in Worship: Essays on the Lord's Supper*. Ed. J.G. Davies and A. Raymond George. (London: Lutterworth Press, 1958), pp. 47-48.

28. *Ibid*, p. 50.

29. In fact, Leenhardt even admitted that transubstantiation was helpful insofar as it expressed these two affirmations about the transformation that occurs in the bread: 1. The substance of things is not in their empirical data, but in the will of God who upholds them. And 2. Jesus Christ declares in the upper room, in a sovereign manner, His will that the bread should be His body; He transforms the substance of this bread. *Ibid*, pp. 49-50.

30. To temper his retention of the term transubstantiation, Leenhardt was adamant in his denial of "static substantialism." As Thomas Dicken points out, "static substantialism" is a danger to any eucharistic theology that is based on the term "substance": "Because substance philosophy suggests a static interpretation of the real presence, it tends to focus attention exclusively on the elements, in abstraction from the total context of the eucharist." To safeguard against this tendency, Leenhardt insisted that the real presence of Christ was not to be found in the bread and wine apart from everything else, but within the total event of the supper and especially within the action of distribution. Transubstantiation, therefore, cannot localize the body of Christ within the elements of the bread. By explaining it in this manner, Leenhardt attempted to go beyond isolating the real presence of Christ in a substance, to the broader context of recognizing it in an action. T.M. Dicken. "Process Philosophy and the Real Presence." *Journal of Ecumenical Studies*. Vol. 6. 1979. p. 73.

31. Leenhardt, 1958, p. 48. A necessary requirement for this change of reality to occur, Leenhardt insisted, is the faith of the person. That is to say that the kind of knowledge that is necessary to comprehend the change in the reality of the bread is possible only to the believer; all the others will consider the change impossible. Thus, only the person of faith will see in the substance of the bread the reality which God wills for it—the real presence of Christ.

32. Grace, according to Schillebeeckx, can be defined as personal saving encounters with God. He explains: "On God's part this encounter involves a disclosure of himself by revelation and on the part of man it involves devo-

tion to God's service—that is, religion. This encounter itself, seen from man's side, is the reality of what is called sanctifying grace." Edward Schillebeeckx. *Christ the Sacrament of the Encounter with God.* (New York: Sheed and Ward, 1963), pp. 4-5.

For a more general discussion on grace in the world, cf. Joseph Fitzer. "Teilhard's Eucharist: A Reflection." *Theological Studies.* Vol. 34. No. 2. June 1963. pp. 251-264.

33. D. Gray. "Sacramental Consciousness-Raising." *Worship.* Vol. 46. 1972. p. 131.

34. Karl Rahner. "How to receive a sacrament and mean it." *Theology Digest.* Vol. 19. 1971. p. 227.

35. *Ibid,* p. 228.

36. Schillebeeckx, 1963, p. 15.

37. Richard Gula. *To Walk Together Again.* (N.Y.: Paulist Press, 1984), p. 74.

38. Karl Rahner. *Foundations of Christian Faith.* (N.Y.: Crossroads, 1984), p. 412. Avery Dulles makes a very good point about this: "The Church does not always signify this equally well. It stands under a divine imperative to make itself a convincing sign. It appears most fully as a sign when its members are evidently united to one another and to God through holiness and mutual love, and when they visibly gather to confess their faith in Christ and to celebrate what God has done for them in Christ." *Models of the Church.* (N.Y.: Doubleday and Co., 1974), p. 72.

39. Schillebeeckx, 1963, p. 51.

40. It is important to point out that despite the emphasis on the Church as the sign which carries on Christ's presence in the world, it is necessary to indicate that such an expanded notion of the sacrament is in no way meant to be exclusive. That is, it does not mean that the Church is an encounter with the saving reality of Christ only for those within. Rather, in accord with the new theology of grace which affirms that the entire world is itself full of grace, the notion of Church as sacrament necessarily involves all people, those who are within the Christian community as well as those who are not. Thus, the Church, as the sign which perpetuates the saving reality of Jesus, far from remaining apart from the world, proclaims to the world that it too is redeemed by its encounter with Jesus. Cf. Rahner, 1971, p. 232.

41. Charles Davis. "Understanding the Real Presence." *The Word in History.* Ed. T. Patrick Burke. (N.Y.: Sheed and Ward, 1966), p. 166.

42. Gula, p. 79.

43. Schillebeeckx, 1968, p. 97. As well, for a good, concise explanation, cf. Thomas Ambrogi. "Sacramental Reality, Sign and Presence." in *Lutherans and Catholics in Dialogue, I-III.* Ed. Paul C. Empie and T. Austin Murphy. (Minneapolis: Augsbury Publishing House, 1974), pp. 182-183.

44. Gula, p. 82.

45. Although various theologians have treated this issue, for the sake of brevity, attention will be focused on the work of Edward Schillebeeckx and, in particular, his book *The Eucharist.* This is not, of course, meant to be by any means exclusive. Certain portions of the work of Schillebeeckx' contemporaries such as Piet Schoonenberg and Charles Davis must be examined in some detail, since this work prepares the ground for, and is used extensively by Schillebeeckx. In placing the dogma of transubstantiation within the

broad context of the eucharist itself, Schillebeeckx relies heavily on the work of Schoonenberg and Davis. "The authentic context in which the Eucharist should be seen has been very suggestively described by Schoonenberg and Davis especially." However, these theologians will be discussed only secondarily, as they apply to and are used by Schillebeeckx. Schillebeeckx, 1968, p. 122.

46. *Ibid*, p. 90.

47. *Ibid*, p. 53.

48. Karl Rahner. "The presence of Christ in the sacrament of the Lord's Supper." *Theological Investigations IV: More Recent Writings*. (London: Darton, Longman and Todd, 1966), p. 303.

49. Kenan Osborne. "Eucharistic Theology Today." *Alternative Futures for Worship: Volume 3—The Eucharist*. Ed. Bernard J. Lee. (Collegeville: Liturgical Press, 1987), p. 97.

50. Piet Schoonenberg. "Presence and the Eucharistic Presence." *Cross Currents*. Vol. 17. Winter 1967. pp. 40-50. I am using Schoonenberg here because, as Schillebeeckx points out, even though Luchesius Smits did a fair amount of work in this area, it follows the same basic direction as that of Schoonenberg's thought. Cf. Schillebeeckx, 1968, pp. 117-121.

51. Powers, p. 121.

52. Schoonenberg, 1967, p. 52.

53. Davis, 1966, p. 169.

54. *Ibid*, p. 160.

55. *Ibid*, p. 170.

56. *Ibid*, p. 162.

57. Charles Davis. "The Theology of Transubstantiation." *Sophia*. Vol. 3. 1964. p. 19.

58. E.L. Mascall. "Eucharistic Doctrine after Vatican II: Some Anglican Anticipations." *Church Quarterly Review*. Vol. 169. April-June, 1968. p. 148.

59. Schillebeeckx, 1968, p. 128.

60. *Ibid*, p. 130.

61. Schillebeeckx' conclusion is well articulated by Joseph Powers. "*Mysterium Fidei* and the theology of the Eucharist." *Worship*. Vol. 40. No. 1. 1966. p. 21.

62. Schillebeeckx, 1968, p. 131.

63. *Ibid*, p. 131.

64. *Ibid*, p. 132.

65. *Ibid*, p. 133.

66. *Ibid*, p. 137.

67. *Ibid*, p. 134.

68. This, according to Mascall, is the principle of transignification: "Transignification does not mean the substitution of one signification or another, but the transformation of one signification into another in which it finds its own fulfillment," p. 155.

69. Phillippe Rouillard. "From Human Meal to Christian Eucharist." *Living Bread, Saving Cup: Readings on the Eucharist*. Ed. R. Kevin Seasoltz. (Collegeville: The Liturgical Press, 1982), p. 132. Kenan Osborne explains it as follows: "The food is part of a meal, but so is the social context and interpersonal sharing which accompanies a meal," 1987, p. 97. For an in-depth de-

scription, cf. Bernard Besret. *Tomorrow a New Church*. (N.Y.: Paulist Press, 1973), pp. 112-115.

70. In her study of Schillebeeckx' work, Marie Zimmerman concludes: "Dans l'eucharistie, la nourriture, le répas et la communauté autour de la table sont unis; c'est la matière humaine qui devient sacrement." Marie Zimmerman. "L'Eucharistie: Quelques Aspects de la Pensée de Schillebeeckx." *Revue des Sciences Religieuses*. Vol. 49. July 1975. p. 239.

71. Schillebeeckx, 1968, p. 137.

72. Paul Jersild. "A Lutheran View of the Real Presence in Roman Catholic Theology Today." *Dialog*. Vol. 12. Spring 1973. p. 139.

73. Schillebeeckx, 1968, p. 139.

74. *Ibid*, p. 139.

75. Schillebeeckx, 1966, p. 337.

76. *Ibid*, p. 337.

77. Schillebeeckx, 1968, pp. 137-138. Piet Schoonenberg concurs with this: ". . . the whole presence of the Lord in his Church—in the celebration of the Eucharist—is important, even more important than his presence in the sacred species alone. Only when we try to plumb the depths of the riches of this presence in community do we find therein the meaning of the real presence under the sacred species." Cf. Schoonenberg, 1967, p. 40.

78. Schillebeeckx, 1968, p. 138.

79. *Ibid*, p. 139.

80. *Ibid*, p. 141.

81. *Ibid*, p. 141.

82. *Ibid*, p. 142.

83. *Ibid*, p. 144.

84. *Ibid*, p. 147. In relation to this, Schillebeeckx maintains that although the way something appears is normally the sign of reality which contains the reality itself, this is not always the case. It is, he claims, "the inadequacy of man's knowledge of reality that accounts for a certain difference between reality and its appearance as a phenomenon."

85. *Ibid*, p. 150. This is well summarized by Powers: "there is a change in the signifying function of these appearances but that change (a 'transsignification') is a change precisely because the reality which is contained in these appearances is no longer the reality of the bread and wine, but Christ's bodily reality." Powers, 1967, p. 153.

86. *Ibid*.

87. Ernest Schoenmaeckers explains that Schillebeeckx had expressed grave doubts about methods that did not clearly state what Trent asked. "Birdcages in Dutch Churches." *America*. Vol. 113. October 1965. p. 408.

88. Peter Beer. "G.B. Sala and E. Schillebeeckx on the eucharistic presence: a critique [transignification and transubstantiation]." *Science et Esprit*. Vol 38. No. 1. Jan-April 1986. p. 34.

Joseph Powers also has a succinct explanation: "What, then, is the meaning of the statement that the change which takes place in the eucharist is a 'transignification'?" Negatively, it does not mean that the believer merely thinks or feels differently about the bread and cup. . . . Positively, it means that God, in the creative power of his word, transforms the religious meaning (the inner value and power) of the unleavened bread and the cup of benediction by fulfilling in Christ all that the bread and cup promised to Israel. In the Eucharist, God transforms the meaning of this bread and cup, giving it a new inner value and power." 1966, p. 30.

89. Jill Raitt. "Roman Catholic Wine in Reformed Old Bottles?" *Journal of Ecumenical Studies*. Vol. 8. 1971. P. 603. Raitt goes on to explain that: "This fundamental inconsistency is avoided by other Roman Catholic authors, e.g. Piet Schoonenberg [who states] '. . . if we consider the finality and the significance themselves as substantial, as given with the reality of the bread and wine and co-constitutive of these elements, then transfinalization and transignification are identical with transubstantiation.'" Quote is from Schoonenberg, 1967, p. 45.

90. Schillebeeckx, 1968, p. 21.

91. Powers, 1966, pp. 29-30.

92. Zimmerman, 1975, p. 245.

93. Pope Paul VI. *Mysterium Fidei*. From *The Papal Encyclicals, 1958-1981*. Ed. Claudia Carlen (McGrath Publishing House, 1981), #1. As Cyril Vollert points out, this same sort of theological discussion had been part of the theological scene for over a decade. For example, while the final form of Schillebeeckx' decisive work, *The Eucharist*, was published in English only in 1967, it was the culmination of many years of work and had already been published in article form in early 1965. That which the encyclical was addressing, then, were these culminated attempts at interpretation. Cyril Vollert. "Transubstantiation and the Encyclical." *Continuum*. Vol. 3. Autumn 1965. p. 388.

94. Donald Campion. "New Trends in Encyclicals." *Commonweal*. Vol. 82. 1965. p. 714.
As well, Joseph Powers claims that "who they are is not mentioned by the Pope, although a segment of the Italian press has dispensed itself from Pope Paul's laudable discretion and focussed its attention on one of the greatest theologians of this age, Prof. E.H. Schillebeeckx." 1966, p. 20.

95. Schoemnaeckers, 1965, p. 408. According to Vilmos Vajta, however, "the denial published in *L'Osservatore Romano* entangled the question still more, since it was misleading." "*Mysterium Fidei*: A Lutheran View." *Concilium*. Vol. 14. 1966. p. 159.

96. René Marlé. "L'encyclique *Mysterium Fidei* sur l'eucharistie." *Etudes*. Vol.323. Novembre, 1965. p. 545.

97. Paul VI, #10.

98. James Quinn. "Interpreting *Mysterium Fidei*." *Month*. Vol. 5. April 1966. p. 206.

99. Paul VI, # 14.

100. Powers, 1966, p. 32.

101. Paul VI, #11.

102. Marlé, 1965, p. 550.

103. Paul VI, #39.

104. *Ibid*, #44.

105. *Ibid*, #46.

106. *Ibid*, #11.

107. *Ibid*, #46.

108. Mascall, p. 149. Joseph Powers agrees with this, stating "what he is rejecting is the contention that 'transignification' or 'transfinalization' are the only
terms in which the theology of the Eucharist can be developed and that the
traditional expression of the church's faith in 'transubstantiation' has no
place in the theology of the Eucharist," 1966, p. 20.

109. Quinn, p. 205.

110. Jersild, p. 137.

111. Schillebeeckx, 1966, p. 325.

Chapter Four

1. Liberation theology is still most clearly enunciated in the so-called Third
    World. However, it is also becoming a factor in the First World. In the
    United States, for example, black theology is becoming more widely known
    and developed. In Europe and North America, theology is becoming in-
    creasingly concerned with the responsibilities of the First World with regard
    to the Third World; problems of ecology and nuclear energy; issues concern-
    ing the 'new poor' (drug addicts, the elderly and migrant workers.) Femin-
    ist theology is also a decisive issue in both the First and the Third World. Cf.
    Leonard and Clodovis Boff. *Introducing Liberation Theology.* (Maryknoll,
    N.Y.: Orbis Books, 1987), p. 81.

    Liberation theology is also overflowing the borders of the church and becom-
    ing a public concern, since it is dealing with social, political and economic
    issues which affect all of society. Leonardo and Clodovis Boff. *Liberation
    Theology: From Confrontation to Dialogue.* (Maryknoll, N.Y.: Orbis Books,
    1986), p. 7.

2. In the earliest days of colonialism, for example, Bartalome de las Casa de-
    voted himself to the defense of the natives by arguing that they had the
    right to be treated as free people. As a result, he is often regarded as a
    prophet of liberation and a forerunner of present day liberation theology.
    Theo Witvliet. *A Place in the Sun: Liberation Theology in the Third World.*
    (Maryknoll, N.Y.: Orbis Books, 1985), p. 11.

3. The Ecumenical Association of Third World Theologians (hereinafter referred
    to as EATWOT) has declared that "theologies from Europe and North Amer-
    ica are dominant today in our churches and represent one form of cultural
    domination." "Why we need a Third World Theology" (London: Catholic
    Institute for International Relations, 1987), p. 16. However, this is beginning
    to change. As Jose Miguez-Bonino explains: "These theologians are increas-
    ingly claiming their right to 'misread' their teachers, to find their own inser-
    tion in the theological tradition, to offer their own interpretation of the
    theological task." *Doing Theology in a Revolutionary Situtation.* (Philadelphia:
    Fortress Press, 1975), p. 62.

4. Boff, 1987, pp. 66-68.

5. Enrique Dussel. *History and the theology of liberation: a Latin American Perspec-
    tive.* (Maryknoll, N.Y.: Orbis Books, 1986), p. 116.

6. "It is within this situation of disillusionment with development that liberation
    theology has emerged . . ." Robert McAfee Brown. "Reflections of Liberation
    Theology." *Religion in Life.* Volume 43. Autumn 1974. p. 270.

7. A.J. Hennelly. *Theologies in Conflict.* (Maryknoll, N.Y.: Orbis Books, 1979), p.
    3.

8. Phillip Berryman. *Liberation Theology: essential facts about the revolutionary movement in Latin America—and beyond.* (Philadelphia: Temple University Press, 1987), p. 22.

9. *Ibid*, p. 12.

10. Brown, 1974, p. 269.

11. Boff, 1987, p. 46.

12. "In the Bible poverty is a scandalous condition inimical to human dignity and therefore contrary to the will of God." Gustavo Gutierrez. *A Theology of Liberation.* (Maryknoll, N.Y.: Orbis Books, 1973), p. 291.

13. Boff, 1987, p. 81.

14. Witvliet, pp. 89-98.

15. Berryman, p. 164.

16. Boff, L. and C., 1986, p. 13. Avery Dulles gives a very helpful definition of the term praxis as it is used in liberation theology. Praxis means ". . . those human activities which are capable of transforming reality and society, and thus of making the world more human. More specifically, praxis is the action that tends to overcome the alienation by which man has become separated from the fruits of his labor. Praxis is therefore revolutionary; it is directed to changing the economic and social relationship. Liberation theologians apply this principle to faith and come up with the Word of God being distorted and alienating whenever it is accepted without commitment to the praxis oriented toward the Kingdom of God." "Faith in Relationship to Justice." *The Faith That Does Justice.* Ed. John C. Haughey. (N.Y.: Paulist Press, 1977).

17. Gutierrez, 1973, p. 15.

18. "Theology itself needs to be 'liberated' from the ivory towers of academies, universities and seminaries. It must take far more account of the experience of faith, and of believers, and confront actual historical reality." Brian Hearne. "Liberation Theology and the Renewal of Theology." *African Ecclesial Review.* Vol. 26. December 1984.
    EATWOT carries this a step further by declaring: "We reject as irrelevant an academic type of theology that is divorced from action. We are prepared for a radical break in epistemology which makes commitment first act of theology and engages in critical reflection on praxis of the reality of the Third World," p. 16.

19. Gustavo Gutierrez. "The Task of Theology and Ecclesial Experience." *Concilium 176: La Iglesia Popular: Between Fear and Hope.* Ed. by Leonardo Boff and Virgil Elizondo. (Edinburgh: T & T Clark, Ltd, 1984), p. 63.

20. This stage is, according to L. Boff, a preliminary, pre-theological stage which is of the utmost importance. Without it, liberation cannot occur and liberation theology cannot be developed. Boff, 1987, pp. 21-22.

21. Gutierrez, 1984, p. 62.

22. Bonino, Jose Miguez. *Room to Be People.* (Philadelphia: Fortress Press, 1979), p. 8.

23. Witzliet, p. 25.

24. Boff, 1987, pp. 24-28.

25. Berryman, p. 87. It is important to note here the term "aid": liberation theologians for the most part have not become involved to any great extent with social theory, but rather, have accepted the premises of social theorists which state that basic structural changes in society are necessary.

26. As quoted in Robert McAfee Brown. *Theology in a New Key*. (Philadelphia: Westminster Press, 1978), p. 67.

27. Witzliet, p. 131. According to Jon Sobrino, the poor rarely consider the dogmas of the Church in their hermeneutical meditations, placing the majority of their emphasis on the Bible. "The 'Doctrinal Authority' of the people of God in Latin America." *Concilium 180: Teaching Authority of Believers*. Ed. by J.B. Metz and Edward Schillebeeckx. (Edinburgh: T & T Clark, Ltd, 1985), p. 57.

28. Boff, 1987, p. 51.

29. Leonardo Boff, *Jesus Christ Liberator*. (Maryknoll, N.Y.: Orbis Books, 1978), p. 279.

30. Dussel, 1987, p. 139.

31. Boff, 1987, p. 40.

32. Brown, 1978, p. 71.

33. This tension is often a major concern for liberation theologians. That is, by over emphasizing the practical, often political, aspect of liberation theology, there is the danger that the core of liberation theology—the spiritual aspect of experiencing God in the suffering of the poor—will be neglected. Boff, 1987, p. 64.

34. Boff, 1987, pp. 11-16.

35. *Ibid*, p. 85.

36. Alvaro Barneiro. *Basic Ecclesial Communities and the Evangelization of the Poor*. (Maryknoll, N.Y.: Orbis Books, 1982), p. 9.

37. Berryman, p. 64. This definition is very broad. There is, as Thomas Bruneau indicates, tremendous variation from diocese to diocese and from country to country. "The Catholic Church and Development in Latin America: the role of Base Christian Communities." *Religious Values and Developments*. Ed. K. Jameson and C. Wilbr, 1980, p. 539.

38. Dussel, p. 165.

39. Most theologians emphatically insist that the base Christian communities are not parallel, clandestine or rebel churches, but rather, a movement of renewal from within the larger church. Cf., for example, Pablo Richard. "The Church of the Poor Within the Popular Movement." *Concilium 176: La Iglesia Popular: Between Fear and Hope*. (Edinburgh: T & T Clark Ltd, 1984), p. 10.
   The base communities do, however, present a challenge to the official church insofar as they hold tremendous implications for the re-definition of the church. Bruneau, p. 540.

40. Berryman, pp. 65-66.

41. Bruneau, p. 537.

42. Leonardo Boff. *Ecclesiogenesis: The Base Communities Reinvent the Church*. (Maryknoll, N.Y.: Orbis Books, 1986), p. 2.

43. Berryman, p. 76.

44. Boff, 1987, p. 5. Cf. also Brown, 1974, p. 272: —"The process of working for change is called conscientization; raising the level of consciousness; perceiving the social, political and economic contradictions in the society; and becoming more and more aware of how truly repressive it is so that action can be undertaken to destroy such structures and bring about liberation."

45. Richard, pp. 10-13.
46. The theology of the sacraments has been dealt with most extensively by Juan Luis Segundo. For that reason, we will rely on his work: *The Sacraments Today*. (Maryknoll, N.Y.; Orbis Books, 1974).
47. Segundo, p. 6.
48. *Ibid*, p. 92.
49. *Ibid*, p. 20.
50. *Ibid*, p. 63.
51. *Ibid*, p. 38.
52. *Ibid*, p. 39.
53. *Ibid*, pp. 79-80.
54. *Ibid*, p. 104.
55. Rafael Avila. *Worship and Politics*. (Maryknoll, N.Y.: Orbis Books, 1981), p. 74. Another indication that the eucharist is not of foremost concern is the amount of literature devoted to it. The Third World theologians dedicate the majority of their efforts to obtaining liberation from a concrete situation. It is usually North American and European writers who deal more exclusively with the eucharist within the context of liberation. For example, Monika Hellwig, Joseph Grassi, Dermot Lane.
56. Dermot Lane. *Foundations for a Social Theology: Praxis, Process and Salvation*. (N.Y.: Paulist Press, 1984), p. 151.
57. A.C. Cochrane. "Eating and Drinking with Jesus." *Christian Century*. Vol. 91. April 10, 1974. p. 392.
58. Lane, p. 151.
59. Tissa Balasuriya. *The Eucharist and Human Liberation*. (Maryknoll, N.Y.: Orbis Books, 1979), p. 2.
60. *Ibid*, p. 57.
61. Lane, p. 143. "Today the trends in the evolution of the eucharistic theology and devotion take place outside the official circles . . .," Balasuriya, p. 39.
62. Balasuriya, p. 11.
63. Joseph A. Grassi. *Broken Bread and Broken Bodies: The Lord's Supper and World Hunger*. (Maryknoll, N.Y.: Orbis Books, 1985), p. 26.
64. Balasuriya, p. 16.
65. Boff, Leonardo. *When Theology Listens to the Poor*. (San Francisco: Harper and Row, 1989), p. 95.
66. Balasuriya, p. 33.
67. R. Kevin Seasoltz. "Justice and the Eucharist." *Worship*. Vol. 58. November 1984. p. 520.
68. Gutierrez, p. 263.
69. Monika Hellwig. *The Eucharist and the Hunger of the World*. (N.Y.: Paulist Press, 1976), p. 10.
70. Paul Abela. "Celebrating and then practicing the Eucharist." *Concilium 109: Charisms in the Church*. Ed. Christian Duquoc and Casiano Floristan. (N.Y.: Seabury Press, 1978), p. 103.
71. Sandra Schneiders. "The Foot Washing (John 13:1-20): An Experiment in Hermeneutics." *The Catholic Biblical Quarterly*. Vol. 43. 1981, p. 87.
72. *Ibid*, p. 81.
73. Lane, p. 149.

74. Avila, p. 93.
75. Boff, *Ecclesiogenesis*, p. 53.
76. Seasoltz, p. 519.
77. Balasuriya, p. 23.
78. Seasoltz, p. 523.
79. John Chrysostom. *Homily 50.* Quoted in Lane, p. 151.
80. Avila, p. 65.
81. Balasuriya, pp. 33-36.
82. *Ibid*, p. 36.
83. *Ibid*, p. 8.
84. Boff, 1989, p. 95.
85. Lane, p. 142.
86. Balasuriya, p. 128. Cf. also Avila, p. 82: "For this reason the Eucharist obliges us to review and renew the commitment we have made to Christ to collaborate with him in the total liberation of all human beings."
87. Lane, p. 144.
88. Boff, 1989, p. 100.
89. Aldo Vannucchi. "Liturgy and Liberation." *International Review of Missions.* Vol. 65. April 1976. pp. 192-193.
90. Segundo Galilea. "Les messes de protestation." *Parole et Mission.* Vol. 14. 1971. p. 334. Rafael Avila, when discussing the protest masses and the article by Galilea seems to take offense at the fact that Galilea seems to consider Protest Masses as "deviations of rebel priests who are imprudent and undisciplined." (p. 85) To the contrary, Avila insists that such Masses ". . . are not deviations but rather challenging liturgical correctives." (p. 86) Protest Masses are, according to Avila, an outline of future Latin American liturgies.
91. Galilea, p. 334.
92. Joseph Gelineau. "Celebrating the Paschal Liberation." *Concilium 92: Politics and Liturgy.* Ed. Herman Schmidt and David Powers. (N.Y.: Herder and Herder, 1974), p. 107.
93. Mahoney, p. 53.
94. Herman Schmidt. "Lines of Political Action in Contemporary Liturgy." *Concilium 92:Politics and Liturgy.* Ed. Herman Schmidt and David Powers. (N.Y.: Herder and Herder, 1974), pp. 18-19.
95. Avila, p. 104.
96. Boff, 1987, p. 64.
97. Vannucchi, p. 191.
98. Jurgen Moltmann. "The Liberating Feast." *Concilium 92: Politics and Liturgy.* Ed. Herman Schmidt and David Power. (N.Y.: Herder and Herder, 1974), p. 79.
   Just world order and kingdom often seem to be used synonymously. Cf. for example, Boff's use: "Kingdom of God . . . means a new world order, where God is all in all." Boff, *Ecclesiogenesis*, p. 51.
99. Avila, p. 100.
100. Gelineau, p. 118.
101. J. Moiser. "Promise of plenty: the eucharist as social critique." *The Downside Review.* Vol. 91. October 1973. p. 305.
102. Brown, 1978, p. 185.

103. Hellwig, p. 12.
104. *Ibid*, p. 18.
105. Grassi, p. 84.
106. Mark Searle. "Serving the Lord with Justice." *Liturgy and Social Justice*. Ed. Mark Searle. (Collegeville, Minnesota: The Liturgical Press, 1980), p. 27. Cf. also Brown, 1978, p. 183.
107. Balasuriya, p. 131.
108. Lane, p. 163. Leonardo Boff expresses this same idea as follows: "the communion of the body and blood of the Lord has real existential meaning only when accompanied by a communion in the social body," 1989, p. 98.
109. Hellwig, p. 80.
110. Walter Burghardt. "Preaching the Just Word." in *Liturgy and Social Justice*. Ed. Mark Searle (Collegeville, Minnesota: The Liturgical Press, 1980), p. 45.
111. Mercy Oduyoye. "The Eucharist as Witness." *International Review of Missions*. Vol. 72. April 1983. p. 227.
112. Balasuriya, p. 131.
113. *Ibid*, p. 39.
114. David Hollenbach. "A Prophetic church and the Catholic Social Imagination." *The Faith That Does Justice*. Ed. John C. Haughey. (N.Y.: Paulist Press, 1977), p. 258.
115. Balasuriya, p. 41.
116. Edward Schillebeeckx. "The Christian Community and its Office Bearers." *Concilium 133: The Right of a Community to a Priest*. Ed. Edward Schillebeeckx and J.B. Metz. (N.Y.: Seabury Press, 1980), p. 126.
117. *Puebla and Beyond*. Ed. John Eagleson and Philip Scharper. (Maryknoll, N.Y.: Orbis Press, 1979), Final Document #662.
118. Balasuriya, p. 117. This shortage of priests is found in most countries. In Latin America, there is 1.8 priests per 10,000 people. Boff, *Ecclesiogenesis*, p. 61.

    Likewise, "the context in which the local churches in Africa usually find themselves is one afflicted by a scarcity of sacramental ministers." Amadeus Msarikie. "The Sacraments are for People." *African Ecclesial Review*. Vol. 20. August 1978. p. 222.
119. Berryman, pp. 78-79.
120. Schillebeeckx, 1980, p. 107.
121. Balasuriya, p. 28.
122. Msarikie, p. 229.
123. Boff, *Ecclesiogenesis*, p. 63.
124. *Ibid*, p. 70.
125. *Ibid*, p. 73.
126. *Ibid*, p. 73.
127. Clodovis Boff. *Feet-on-the-Ground Theology*. (Maryknoll, N.Y.: Orbis Books, 1984), p. 133.
128. Robert McAfee Brown. "The Roman Curia and Liberation Theology: the second and final round." *Christian Century*. Vol. 103. June 4-11, 1986. p. 552.
129. Berryman, p. 109.
130. Brown, 1986, p. 554.

131. According to Juan Luis Segundo, that which is being attacked in the *Instruction* is simply a caricature of liberation theology in which no liberation theologian of any standing would recognize himself (pp. 8-13). Furthermore, Segundo concludes, it is not only liberation theology that is being attacked in the *Instruction*, but the whole of Vatican II and post-conciliar theology. (pp. 155-156) *Theology and the Church: A Response to Cardinal Ratzinger and a Warning to the Whole Church.* (N.Y.: Seabury Press, 1985).

132. "Instruction on Certain Aspects of the "Theology of Liberation." *Origins.* September 13, 1984. Volume 14. VI, 4.

133. *Ibid,* IV, 15.

134. *Ibid,* IX, 13.

135. *Ibid,* introduction.

136. *Ibid,* VIII, 6.

137. *Ibid,* IX, 10.

138. *Ibid,* X, 16.

139. *Ibid.*

140. Boff, 1989, p. 102.

141. John McKenna. "Liturgy: Toward Liberation or Oppression?" *Worship.* Vol. 56. July 1982. p. 299.

Chapter Five

1. Charles Davis. "Understanding the Real Presence." in *The Word in History.* Ed. T. Patrick Burke. (N.Y.: Sheed and Ward, 1966), p. 155. In addition, one must also take into account the fact that history also shapes theological renewal; changes in theology are always conditioned by outside factors. Theology cannot, therefore, remain outside or apart from the progress of history.

2. It is highly likely that these two reinterpretations are not totally unrelated. The reinterpretation of the eucharist in liberation theology, which came about later, undoubtedly was influenced by Schillebeeckx' work, especially his emphasis on community and the multiple presence of Christ in the liturgy. Many of the liberation theologians who deal with eucharistic theology studied in Europe where they no doubt came into contact with Schillebeeckx' writings. On the other hand, it is also highly plausible that Schillebeeckx' later work on alternative ways of celebrating the eucharist gained something from those practices which were already in place in many areas of Latin America from whence liberation theology arose. Hence, one can speculate that the two re-interpretations had, to some extent, an influence on each other.

3. Abela, Paul. "Celebrating and then practicing the Eucharist." in *Concilium* 109: *Charisms in the Church.* Ed. Christian Duquoc and Casiano Floristan. (N.Y.: Seabury Press, 1978), p. 100.

4. Arthur Cochrane. "Eating and Drinking with Jesus." *Christian Century.* Volume 91. April 10, 1974. p. 392. Cf. Chapter 4, Footnote 57.

5. Aldo Vannuchi. "Liturgy and Liberation." *International Review of Missions.* Vol. 65. April 1976. p. 189.

6. Joseph M. Powers. "Eucharist: symbol of freedom and community," in *Christian Spirituality in the United States.* Ed. F. Eigo. 1978. p. 208.

7. Quoted from Sean McDonagh. *To Care for the Earth*, in "Here Rice is Holier than Wheat." in *National Catholic Reporter*. March 10, 1989.

8. "Constitution on the Sacred Liturgy," #26, in *The Documents of Vatican II*. Ed. Walter M. Abbott. (N.Y.: Guild Press, 1966).

9. Schillebeeckx, Edward. *The Eucharist*. (N.Y.: Sheed and Ward, 1968), p. 125.

10. Liberation theology also carries the notion of the multiple presence of Christ one step further. While both Vatican II and Schillebeeckx recognized and acknowledged Christ's presence in the whole of the eucharistic liturgy, including the gathered assembly, liberation theologians are now expanding this concept beyond the boundaries of the church community and its liturgies. That is, they insist on acknowledging Christ's presence in other people, especially the poor, in a very real way. Many of these theologians maintain that Christ's presence in the eucharist is the same as, and therefore must complement, Christ's presence in the poor. As a result, the church community cannot choose to revere the one and ignore the other. Cf., for example, Dermot Lane. *Foundations for a Social Theology: Praxis, Process and Salvation*. (N.Y.: Paulist Press, 1984), p. 155.

11. Avery Dulles. *Models of the Church*. (N.Y.: Doubleday and Co., Inc., 1974).

12. Richard McBrien. *Church: The Continuing Quest*. (Paranus, N.Y.: Newman Press, 1970), p. 61. Quoted in Dulles, p. 78.

13. E. J. Kilmartin. "Sacramental Theology: the Eucharist in Recent Literature." *Theological Studies*. Vol. 32. June 1971. p. 263.

14. R. Kevin Seasoltz. "Justice and the Eucharist." *Worship*. Vol. 58. November 1984. p. 520.

15. Penny Lernoux. *People of God: The Struggle for World Catholicism*. (N.Y.: Viking Penguin, Inc., 1989), p. 9.

16. While it is true that Schillebeeckx' reinterpretation is found wanting in this dimension of service, this is not necessarily a major defect. In his defense, it must be acknowledged that this dimension was almost unheard of at the time when he was writing. Most importantly, his reinterpretation seeks to put eucharistic theology into more personal, human categories of meaning and significance. This shift in emphasis from an objective concentration on the elements of bread and wine to a subjective focus on the meaning of these elements for the individual believer was a necessary change. I would argue that this focus on self is a prerequisite to being able to focus on others. That is to say that the eucharist *must* be meaningful and able to affect a person on a personal level before that person can go beyond self to others in service and outreach. It is necessary, therefore, to first interiorize the meaning of the eucharist before being able to put that meaning into action beyond oneself.

17. "Schillebeeckx has written with some regularity on church ministry since the mid-1950's. His understanding of ministry has evolved with his understanding of church. Some of his views became widely known on the basis of his book on clerical celibacy in the latter part of the 1960's. But it was especially his book *Ministry* which brought his views to world attention." *The Schillebeeckx Reader*. Ed. Robert Schreiter. (N.Y.: Crossroad Publishers, 1984), p. 220.

18. CORPUS Canada Journal. November 1989. p. 5.

19. Ibid, p. 4.

20. Joan Chittister. *Winds of Change: Women Challenge the Church*. (Kansas City: Sheed & Ward, 1986), p. 88.

21. Quoted in Chapter 4, p. 124.

22. Edward Schillebeeckx. *Ministry: Leadership in the Community of Jesus Christ*. (N.Y.: Crossroad Publishing Co., 1981), p. 29-30.

23. Richard Szafranski. "The One Who Presides at the Eucharist." *Worship*. Vol. 63. No. 4. July 1989. p. 311.

24. Edward Schillebeeckx. *The Church with a Human Face: A New and Expanded Theology of Ministry*. (N.Y.: Crossroad, 1987), p. 256-257.

25. *Ibid*, p. 258.

26. Ad Willems. "The Case of Edward Schillebeeckx." in *The Church in Anguish*. Ed. by Hans Kung and Leonard Swidler. (San Francisco: Harper and Row, Inc., 1987), p. 219-221.

27. Schillebeeckx, 1987, p. 255.

28. "Decree on Ecumenism." in *The Documents of Vatican II*. Ed. Walter Abbott. (New Jersey: New Century Publishers, 1966), Art. #4.

29. Osborne, 1987, p. 102.

30. Paul Jersild. "A Lutheran View of the Real Presence in Roman Catholic Theology Today." *Dialog*. 12 (Spring 1973), p. 139.

31. *Ibid*, p. 140.

32. In Vatican II's *Decree on Ecumenism*, for example, it is declared that while non-Catholics do not have access to the fullest possible means of grace in the eucharistic celebrations, grace is nevertheless conveyed through the sacred actions. As A. Bea points out, while the decree does not specify exactly what these sacred actions are, "it would be difficult not to infer that they include the very centre of Christian worship." Augustin Bea. *The Way to Unity After the Council*. New York: Herder and Herder, 1967. p.147.

33. Leonardo Boff. *Ecclesiogenesis: Base Communities Reinvent the Church*. (Maryknoll: Orbis, 1987), p. 64.

34. Hastings, p. 136.

35. Phillippe Rouillard. "From Human Meal to Christian Eucharist," in *Living Bread, Saving Cup: Readings on the Eucharist*. Ed. R. Kevin Seasoltz. (Collegeville, Minn.: The Liturgical Press, 1982), p. 132.

36. Quoted from Sean McDonagh. *To Care for the Earth, in "Here Rice is Holier than Wheat," in National Catholic Reporter*. March 10, 1989.

37. Lernoux, p. 412. Lernoux here is quoting Marie Dominique Chenu.

38. Boff, *Ecclesiogenesis*, p. 63.

39. "Officials say Document to have wide effect," in *National Catholic Reporter*. February 9, 1990. p. 7. It could be argued that since the *Catechism* is intended for those bishops who have the task of composing and approving national catechisms, there is little danger that it will have an effect on the large, majority of Catholics. To the contrary, however, this document would have a tremendous impact on all Catholics. It will be used as the norm from which to judge national catechisms. In terms of the statement that the eucharist is not a meal, then, the implications are, according to some critics, evident: "If it stays in the final revision, it will be used by pressure groups to label entire catechetical programs as unfaithful to the Universal Catechism." Francis Buckley. Quoted in "Officials say document to have wide effect,' in *National Catholic Reporter*. February 9, 1990, p. 7. As well, there is some speculation that the catechism

will be used as a tool to discipline theologians and scholars. (Hollenbach. Quoted in "Catechism draft roundly criticized" by Jerry Filteau. *Prairie Messenger*. January 15, 1990. p. 5). Thus, in both cases, it is evident that the catechism will ensure that that which is taught is traditional eucharistic doctrine.

40. Pat Windsor. "World's bishops get Universal Catechism but have little time to consult, respond," in *National Catholic Reporter*. January 12, 1990, p. 9.

Bibliography

Abela, Paul. "Celebrating and then practicing the Eucharist." *Concilium 109: Charisms in the Church.* Ed. Christian Duquoc and Casiano Floristan. New York: Seabury Press, 1978.

Ambrogi. T. "Contemporary Roman Catholic theology of the eucharistic sacrifice: sacramental reality, sign and presence." *Lutherans and Catholics in Dialogue, I-III.* Ed. Paul C. Empie and T. Austin Murphy. Minneapolis: Augsbury Publishing House, 1974.

Aquinas, Thomas. *Summa Theologiae.* Latin text and English translation; introductions, notes, appendices, glossaries. Blackfriars. London: Eyre and Spottiswoode; New York: McGraw-Hill Book Co., 1964.

Assman, Hugo. *Theology for a Nomad Church.* Trans. Paul Burns. Maryknoll, New York: Orbis Books, 1976.

Avila, Rafael. *Worship and Politics.* Maryknoll, New York: Orbis Books, 1981.

Balasuriya, Tissa. *The Eucharist and Human Liberation.* Maryknoll, New York: Orbis Books, 1979.

Barneiro, Alvaro. *Basic Ecclesial Communities and the Evangelization of the Poor.* Maryknoll, New York: Orbis Books, 1982.

Bea, Augustin. *The Way to Unity After the Council.* New York: Herder and Herder, 1967.

Beer, Peter. "G.B. Sala and E. Schillebeeckx on the eucharistic presence; a critique [transignification and transubstantiation]." *Science et Esprit.* Volume 38. Number 1. January-April 1986.

Berryman, Phillip. *Liberation Theology: essential facts about the revolutionary movement in Latin America—and beyond.* Philadelphia: Temple University Press, 1987.

Besret, Bernard. *Tomorrow a New Church.* New York: Paulist Press, 1973.

Boff, Clodovis. *Feet-on-the-Ground Theology.* Maryknoll, New York: Orbis Books, 1984.

———. and Boff, Leonardo. *Introducing Liberation Theology.* Maryknoll, New York: Orbis Books, 1987.

———. *Liberation Theology: From Confrontation to Dialogue.* Maryknoll, New York: Orbis Books, 1986.

Boff, Leonardo. "A Theological Examination of the terms 'People of God' and 'Popular Church.'" *Concilium 176: La Iglesia Popular: Between Fear and Hope.* Ed. Leonardo Boff and Virgil Elizondo. Edinburgh: T & T Clark, Ltd., 1984.

———. *Ecclesiogenesis: Base Communities Reinvent the Church.* Maryknoll, New York: Orbis Books, 1987.

———. *Jesus Christ Liberator.* Trans. Patrick Hughes. Maryknoll, New York: Orbis Books, 1978.

———. *When Theology Listens to the Poor.* San Francisco: Harper and Row, 1989.

Bokenkotter, Thomas. *A Concise History of the Catholic Church.* Garden City, N.Y.: Image Books, 1979.

Bonino, Jose-Miquez. *Doing Theology in a Revolutionary Situation.* Philadelphia: Fortress Press, 1975.

————. *Room to be People.* Philadelphia: Fortress Press, 1979.

Bouyer, Louis. *The Liturgy Revived: A Doctrinal Commentary of the Conciliar Constitution on the Liturgy.* Notre Dame, Indiana: University of Notre Dame Press, 1964.

Bradley, Robert and Kevane, Eugene. *The Roman Catechism.* Trans. and annotated in Accord with Vatican II and Post-Conciliar Documents and the New Code of Canon Law. Boston, Massachusetts: St. Paul Editions, 1985.

Brown, Robert McAfee. "Reflections on Liberation Theology." *Religion in Life.* Volume 43. Autumn 1974.

————. "The Roman Curia and Liberation Theology: the second and final round." *Christian Century.* Volume 103. Number 19. June 4-11 1986.

————. *Theology in a New Key.* Philadelphia: Westminster Press, 1978.

Bruneau, Thomas C. "The Catholic church and development in Latin America: the role of the base Christian communities." *Religious Values and Development.* Ed. K. Jameson and C. Wilbr, 1980.

Burghardt, Walter. "Preaching the Just Word." *Liturgy and Social Justice.* Ed. Mark Searle. Collegeville, Minnesota: The Liturgical Press, 1980.

Campion, Donald. "New Trends in Encyclicals." *Commonweal.* Volume 82. October 1, 1965.

Catechism of the Council of Trent for Parish Priests. Translated and Notes by John A. McHugh and Charles Callan. Indiana: Marian Publishers, 1972.

Chemnitz, Martin. *Examination of the Council of Trent.* St. Louis: Concordia Publishing House, 1971.

Chittister, Joan. *Winds of Change: Women Challenge the Church.* Kansas City: Sheed and Ward, 1986.

Cipolla, Richard G. "Selvaggi revisited: Transubstantiation and Contemporary Science." *Theological Studies.* Volume 35. Number 4. December 1974.

Clarke, Francis. *Eucharistic Sacrifice and the Reformation.* London: Darton, Longmann and Todd, Ltd, 1960.

Cochrane, A.C. "Eating and Drinking with Jesus." *Christian Century.* Volume 91. April 10, 1974.

CORPUS Canada Journal. November 1989.

Davis, Charles. "The Theology of Transubstantiation." *Sophia.* Volume 3. 1964.

————. "Understanding the Real Presence." *The Word in History.* Ed. T. Patrick Burke. New York: Sheed and Ward, 1966.

De Baciocchi, J. *L'Eucharistie.* Tournai, Belgium: Desclée and Co., 1961.

————. "Présence eucharistique et transsubstantiation" *Irénikon.* Volume 32. 1959.

De Montcheuil, Yves. "La raison de la permanence du Christ sous les espèces eucharistiques d'après Bonaventure et Thomas." *Mélanges Théologiques: Série Théologie n.9.* Paris: Editions du Cerf, 1946.

Denzinger. *The Sources of Catholic Dogma*. Trans. Roy DeLerrari. London: B. Herder Book Co. 1957.

Dicken, T. M. "Process Philosophy and the Real Presence." *Journal of Ecumenical Studies*. Volume 6. 1969.

Diederich, Everett. "Reflections on post-conciliar shifts in eucharistic faith and practice." *Communio (US)*. Volume 12. Summer 1985.

———. "The unfolding presence of Christ in the Mass." *Communio (US)*. Winter 1978.

Documents of Vatican II, The. Ed. Walter M. Abbott. New Jersey: New Century Publishers, Inc., 1966.

Documents on the Liturgy, 1963-1979: Conciliar, Papal and Curial Texts. Collegeville, Minnesota: The Liturgical Press, 1982.

Dulles, Avery. "Faith in Relationship to Justice." *The Faith That Does Justice*. Ed. John C. Haughey. New York: Paulist Press, 1977.

———. *Models of the Church*. New York: Doubleday and Co., Inc., 1974.

Dussel, Enrique. *History and the theology of liberation: a Latin American perspective*. Trans. John Drury. Maryknoll, New York: Orbis Books, 1976.

———. "The bread of eucharistic celebration as a sign of justice in the community." *Concilium 152: Can we always celebrate the Eucharist?* Ed. M. Collins. New York: Seabury Press, 1982.

Ecumenical Association of Third World Theologians. "Why we need a Third World Theology." London: Catholic Institute for International Relations, 1987.

"*Eucharisticum Mysterium*." *Vatican II: The Conciliar and Post-Conciliar Documents*. Ed. Austin Flannery. Wilmington, Delaware: Scholarly Resources Inc., 1975.

Filteau, Jerry. "Catechism draft roundly criticized." *Prairie Messenger*. January 15, 1990.

Fink, Peter E. "Perceiving the presence of Christ." *Worship*. Volume 58. January 1984.

Fitzer, Joseph. "Teilhard's Eucharist: A Reflection." *Theological Studies*. Volume 34. Number 2. June 1973.

Fullam, Raymond B. *Exploring Vatican II: Christian Living Today and Tomorrow*. Montreal: Palm Publishers, 1969.

Galilea, Segundo. "Les messes de protestation." *Parole et Mission*. Volume 14. 1971.

Gelineau, Joseph. "Celebrating the Paschal Liberation." in *Concilium 92: Politics and Liturgy*. Ed. Herman Schmidt and David Power. New York: Herder and Herder, 1974.

Ghysens, G. "Présence réele et transsubstantiation dans les definitions de l'Eglise Catholique." *Irénikon*. Volume 32. 1959.

Gihr, Nicolas. *The Holy Sacrifice of the Mass*. St. Louis: B. Herder Book Co., 1949.

Gonzalez, Justo. *A History of Christian Thought*. Nashville: Abingdon Press, 1971.

Grassi, Joseph A. *Broken Bread and Broken Bodies: The Lord's Supper and World Hunger.* Maryknoll, New York: Orbis Press, 1985.

Gray, D. "Sacramental Consciousness-Raising." *Worship.* Volume 46. 1972.

Green, H. Benedict. "The Eucharistic Presence: Change and/or signification." *The Downside Review.* Volume 83. 1965.

Gula, Richard. *To Walk Together Again.* New York: Paulist Press, 1984.

Gutierrez, Gustavo. *A Theology of Liberation.* Maryknoll, New York: Orbis Books, 1973.

————. "The Task of Theology and Ecclesial Experience." *Concilium* 176: La Iglesia Popular: Between Fear and Hope. Ed. Leonardo Boff and Virgil Elizonda. Edinburgh: T & T Clark, Ltd., 1984.

Hastings, Adrian. *A Concise Guide to the Documents of Vatican II.* London: Darton, Longmann and Todd, 1968.

Hawkins, D.J.B. "Reflections on Transubstantiation." *The Downside Review.* Volume 80. 1962.

Hearne, Brian. "Liberation Theology and the Renewal of Theology." *African Ecclesial Review.* Volume 26. December 1984.

Hellwig, Monika. *The Eucharist and the Hunger of the World.* New York: Paulist Press, 1976.

Hennelly, A. J. (ed) *Theologies in Conflict.* Maryknoll, N.Y.: Orbis Books, 1979.

"Here Rice is Holier Than Wheat." in *National Catholic Reporter.* March 10, 1989.

Herzog, F. L. "Origins of Liberation Theology." *Duke Divinity Review.* Volume 38. Fall 1973.

Hollenbach, David. "A Prophetic Church and the Catholic Social Imagination." *The Faith That Does Justice.* Ed. John C. Haughey. New York: Paulist Press, 1977.

Hughes, John. "Eucharistic Sacrifice: Transcending the Reformation Deadlock." *Worship.* Volume 43. Number 9.

"Instruction on Certain Aspects of Liberation Theology." *Origins.* Volume 14. September 13, 1984.

Jedin, Hubert. *Crisis and Closure of the Council of Trent: A Retrospective View From the Second Vatican Council.* Trans. N.D. Smith. London: Sheed and Ward, 1967.

Jersild, Paul. "A Lutheran View of the Real Presence in Roman Catholic theology." *Dialog.* Volume 12. Spring 1973.

Jungmann, Josef. "Commentary on the Constitution on the Sacred Liturgy." *Commentary on the Documents of Vatican II.* Ed. Herbert Vorgrimler. New York: Herder and Herder, 1967.

Kee, Alistair. "Authority and Liberation: conflict between Rome and Latin America [Boff-Ratzinger confrontation]." *Modern Churchman.* Volume 28. Number 1. 1985.

Kiesling, Christopher. "Roman Catholic and Reformed Understandings of the Eucharist." *Journal of Ecumenical Studies.* Volume 13. Spring 1976.

Kilmartin, Edward J. "Christ's Presence in the Liturgy." *Bread From Heaven.* Ed. Paul Bernier. New York: Paulist Press, 1977.

————. "Sacramental Theology: The Eucharist in Recent Literature." *Theological Studies*. Volume 32. June 1971.

Lane, Dermot A. *Foundations for a Social Theology: Praxis, Process and Salvation*. New York: Paulist Press, 1984.

Leenhardt, F.J. "This is My Body." *Ecumenical Studies in Worship: Essays on the Lord's Supper*. Ed. J. G. Davies and A. Raymond George. London: Lutterworth Press, 1958.

Lernoux, Penny. *People of God: The Struggle for World Catholicism*. New York: Viking Penguin, Inc., 1989.

Lindbeck, George A. *The Future of Roman Catholic Theology: Vatican II-Catalyst for Change*. Philadelphia: Fortress Press, 1970.

Luther, Martin. *Luther's Works*. Volumes 35-38. Ed. Helmut T. Lehmenn. Philadelphia: Fortress Press, 1951ff.

McBrien, Richard. *Catholicism*. San Francisco: Harper and Row, 1981.

McCue, James F. "The Doctrine of Transubstantiation from Berengar through the Council of Trent." *Lutherans and Catholics in Dialogue, I-III*. Ed. Paul C. Empie and T. Austin Murphy. Minneapolis: Augsburg Publishing House, 1967.

McDonald, Allan J. *Berengar and the Reform of Sacramental Doctrine*. Merrick, New York: Richwood Publishing Co., 1977.

McDonnell, Kilian. *John Calvin, the Church and the Eucharist*. Princeton, New Jersey: Princeton University Press, 1967.

McKenna, John H. "Liturgy: Toward Liberation or Oppression?" *Worship*. Volume 56. July 1982.

MacEoin, Gary. *What Happened at Rome? The Council and its Implications for the Modern World*. New York: Echo Book, 1967.

Mahoney, Roger. "The Eucharist and Social Justice." *Worship*. Volume 57. January 1983.

Manus, Chris U. "The Eucharist: a neglected factor in contemporary theology of liberation." *African Ecclesial Review*. Volume 27. August 1985.

Marle, Rene. "L'encyclique *Mysterium Fidei* sur l'Eucharistie." *Etudes*. Volume 323. Novembre 1965.

Martelet, Gustave. *The Risen Christ and the Eucharistic World*. Trans. Rene Hague. New York: Seabury Press, 1976.

Martos, Joseph. *Doors to the Sacred: A Historical Introduction to Sacraments in the Catholic Church*. Garden City, New York: Doubleday and Co., Inc., 1981.

Mascall, E.L. "Eucharistic doctrine after Vatican II; some Anglican anticipations." *Church Quarterly Review*. Volume 169. January-March; April-June 1968.

Michel, A. "L'encyclique *Mysterium Fidei* et les deviations doctrinales sur l'eucharistie." *L'Ami du Clerge*. Volume 75. 1965.

Mikloshazy, Attila. "Commentary on the Constitution on the Sacred Liturgy." *The Church Renewed: The Documents of Vatican II Reconsidered*. Ed. George P. Schner. New York: University Press of America, 1986.

Moiser, J. "Promise of plenty: the Eucharist as social critique." *The Downside Review*. Volume 91. October 1973.

Moltmann, Jurgen. "The Liberating Feast." *Concilium 92: Politics and Liturgy.* Ed. Herman Schmidt and David Power. New York: Herder and Herder, 1974.

Msarikie, Amedeus. "The sacraments are for people." *African Ecclesial Review.* Volume 20. August 1978.

Oduyoye, Mercy Amba. "The Eucharist as Witness." *International Review of Missions.* Volume 72. Number 286. April 1983.

"Officials Say Document to have Wide Spread Effect." *National Catholic Reporter.* February 9, 1990.

O'Neill, Colman. "The Role of the Recipient and Sacramental Signification." *Thomist.* Volume 21. 1958.

Osborne, Kenan. "Contemporary Understandings of the Eucharist: A Survey of Catholic Thinking." *Journal of Ecumenical Studies.* Volume 13. Number 2. Spring 1979.

———. "Eucharistic Theology Today." *Alternative Futures for Worship. Volume 3: The Eucharist.* Ed. Bernard J. Lee. Collegeville: The Liturgical Press, 1987.

Paul VI, Pope. *Mysterium Fidei. The Papal Encyclicals: 1958-1981.* Ed. Claudia Carlen. McGrath Publishing House, 1981.

Pelikan, Jaroslav. *Reformation of Church and Dogma (1300-1700).* Chicago: University of Chicago Press, 1984.

———. *The Growth of Medieval Theology (600-1300).* Chicago: University of Chicago Press, 1978.

Pius XII, Pope. *Mediator Dei. The Papal Encyclicals in their Historical Context.* Ed. Anne Fremantle. New York: New American Library, 1956.

Powers, Joseph M. "Eucharist: Symbol of Freedom and Community." *Christian Spirituality in the United States.* Ed. F. Eigo. 1978.

———. *Eucharistic Theology.* New York: Herder and Herder, 1967.

———. "*Mysterium Fidei* and the theology of the Eucharist." *Worship.* Volume 40. Number 1. 1966.

Puebla and Beyond. Ed. John Eagleson and Phillip Scharper. New York: Orbis Press, 1979.

Purday, K.M. "Berengar and the Use of the Word 'Substantia.' " *The Downside Review.* Volume 19. Number 303. April 1973.

Quinn, James. "Interpreting *Mysterium Fidei.*" *Month.* Volume 5. April 1966.

Rahner, Karl. "How to receive a sacrament and mean it." *Theology Digest.* Volume 19. 1971.

———. *Meditation on the Sacraments.* New York: Seabury Press, 1977.

———. *The Church and the Sacraments.* Freiburg: Herder, 1963.

———. "The Presence of Christ in the Sacrament of the Lord's Supper." *Theological Investigations IV: More Recent Writings.* London: Darton, Longman and Todd, 1966.

Raitt, Jill. "Roman Catholic Wine in Reformed Old Bottles?" *Journal of Ecumenical Studies.* Volume 8. 1971.

Rouillard, Phillipe. "From Human Meal to Christian Eucharist." *Living Bread, Saving Cup: Readings on the Eucharist.* Ed. R. Kevin Sezsoltz. Collegeville, Minnesota: The Liturgical Press, 1982.

Schneiders, Sandra M. "The Foot Washing (John 13:1-20): An Experiment in Hermeneutics." *The Catholic Biblical Quarterly*. Volume 43. 1981.

Schillebeeckx, Edward. *Christ the Sacrament of the Encounter with God.* New York: Sheed and Ward, 1963.

———. *Ministry: Leadership in the Community of Jesus Christ.* New York: Crossroad Publishing Co., 1981.

———. "The Christian Community and its Office Bearers." *Concilium 133: The Right of a Community to a Priest.* Ed. Edward Schillebeeckx and J.B. Metz. New York: Seabury Press, 1980.

———. *The Church with a Human Face: A New and Expanded Theology of Ministry.* New York: Crossroad Publishing Company, 1987.

———. *The Eucharist.* New York: Sheed and Ward, 1968.

———. *The Schillebeeckx Reader.* Ed. Robert Schreiter. New York: Crossroad Publishers, 1984.

———. "Transubstantiation, Transfinalization, Transfiguration." *Worship.* Volume 40. Number 6. 1966.

Schmidt, Herman. "Lines of Political Action in Contemporary Liturgy." *Concilium 92: Politics and Liturgy.* Ed. Herman Schmidt and David Power. New York: Herder and Herder, 1974.

Schoenmaeckers, E. "Birdcages in Dutch Churches: *Mysterium Fidei* on the Eucharist in light of modern theology." *America.* Volume 113. October 9, 1965.

Schoonenberg, Piet. "Presence and the Eucharistic Presence." *Cross Currents.* Volume 17. Winter 1967.

———. "Transubstantiation: How Far is this Doctrine Historically Determined?" *Concilium 24: The Sacraments: An Ecumenical Dilemma.* Ed. Hans Kung. New York: Paulist Press, 1967.

Searle, Mark. "Serving the Lord with Justice." *Liturgy and Social Justice.* Ed. Mark Searle. Collegeville, Minnesota: The Liturgical Press, 1980.

Seasoltz, R. Kevin. "Justice and the Eucharist." *Worship.* Volume 58. November 1984.

Segundo, Juan Luis. *The Sacraments Today.* Maryknoll, New York: Orbis Books, 1974.

———. *Theology and the Church: A Response to Cardinal Ratzinger and a Warning to the Whole Church.* Trans. John Dierchsmeier. Minneapolis: Winston Press, 1985.

Sobrino, Jon. "The 'Doctrinal Authority' of the People of God in Latin America." *Concilium 180: The Teaching Authority of Believers.* Ed. J.B. Metz and Edward Schillebeeckx. Edinburgh: T & T Clark, Ltd, 1985.

Steinmetz, David. "Scripture and the Lord's Supper in Luther's Theology." *Interpretation.* Volume 37. Number 3. July 1983.

Szafranski, Richard. "The One Who Presides at the Eucharist." *Worship.* Volume 63. Number 4. July 1989.

Vajta, Vilmos. "*Mysterium Fidei*: A Lutheran View." *Concilium 14.* 1966.

Vannucchi, Aldo. "Liturgy and Liberation." *International Review of Missions.* Volume 65. April 1976.

Verheul, A. *Introduction to the Liturgy*. Collegeville, Minnesota: The Liturgical Press, 1968.

Vollert, Cyril. "The Eucharist: Controversy on Transubstantiation." *Theological Studies*. Volume 22. 1961.

Vollert, Cyril. "Transubstantiation and the Encyclical." *Continuum*. Volume 3. Autumn 1965.

Walsh, Liam. "The Sacraments and Sacramentals." *Vatican II: The Liturgical Constitution*. Ed. Austin Flannery. Dublin: Scepter Books, 1964.

Willems, Ad. "The Case of Edward Schillebeeckx." *The Church in Anguish*. Ed. Hans Kung and Leonard Swidler. San Francisco: Harper and Row, Inc. 1987.

Windsor, Pat. "World's bishops get Universal Catechism but have little time to consult, respond." *National Catholic Reporter*. January 12, 1990.

Witzliet, Theo. *A Place in the Sun: Liberation Theology in the Third World*. Maryknoll, New York: Orbis Books, 1985.

Zimmerman, Marie. "L'Eucharistie: Quelques Aspects de la Pensée de Schillebeeckx." *Revue des Sciences Religieuses*. Volume 49. July 1975.

Index